PETER H

SUPERNATURAL

~ BRITAIN ~

A Guide to Britain's
Most Haunted Places

Other books by Peter Hough

Witchcraft: A Strange Conflict
The Afterlife: An Investigation into the
Mysteries of Life After Death
(with Jenny Randles)
The Complete Book of UFOs
(with Jenny Randles)
Strange But True?
(with Jenny Randles)

PETER HOUGH

SUPERNATURAL
~ BRITAIN ~

*A Guide to Britain's
Most Haunted Places*

PIATKUS

ACKNOWLEDGEMENTS

I should like to thank the following individuals and organizations for their assistance in researching and preparing this book:

Gay Baldwin, Colin Barton, Jennifer Brand, David Clarke, Lynton Fellows, Gwasg Carreg Gwalch, John Humphries, Steven Ironmonger, Robin Laurance, Dewi Lewis, Malcolm Robinson, the Revd Jonathan Russell, Dean Swift, the British Tourist Authority, the Forestry Commission, the Friends of Highgate Cemetery, Livingston Development Corporation, the *Western Mail* and the *Wrexham Leader*. I would also like to thank Anne and Gill at Piatkus for their enthusiasm. Tough task masters they may be, but who am I to argue – a mere man? Their ideas and suggestions enhanced my original proposal.

©1995 Peter Hough

First published in 1995 by
July Piatkus (Publishers) Ltd of
5 Windmill Street, London W1P 1HF

First paperback edition 1995

A catalogue record of this book is
available from the British Library

ISBN 0-7499-1406-8
0-7499-1507-2 (pbk)

Edited by Esther Jagger
Designed by Chris Warner
Maps by Dick Vine
Illustrations by Philip Hood/Arena
Photograph 1, Mary Evans Picture Library; 2, 3 and 4, Peter Hough;
5–12 Janet and Colin Bord/Fortean Picture Library;
13, P.A. Macnab/Camera Press, London.

Set in Meridien Roman by
Create Publishing Services Ltd., Bath, Avon
Printed and bound in Great Britain by
The Bath Press, Avon

Contents

Introduction
1

NORTH-WEST ENGLAND

NORTH-EAST ENGLAND

SOUTH-EAST ENGLAND

SCOTLAND

Introduction

WELCOME to *Supernatural Britain*. This book has grown out of twenty years' research and field investigation into the Unknown. It is also the consequence of a piece of advice I was given many years ago.

During one of my trips to Loch Ness, when I made my usual visit to the camp of investigator Frank Searle at Lower Foyers, he said something which struck home. Despite his dubious photographs of the monster, Searle spoke a lot of sense about the loch and other things too. On this occasion I was interviewing him for an article I was to write.

'Peter,' he said, 'instead of writing about *my* experiences, why don't you get out there and experience things yourself? Do your own thing, then write about that.'

Several years later I was interviewing London psychic Peter Lee when he told me: 'Someone said to you, "You should go and get some experience." I don't know why, but it seems important.' It *was* important. I became more directly involved, and slowly expanded my field investigations to include all areas of the paranormal. Without sacrificing my objectivity it gave me a healthy respect for those who have experienced things which make a nonsense of our concept of 'reality' – of what the consensus of opinion dictates can and cannot be.

Today I am chairman of the Northern Anomalies Research Organisation (NARO) and a member of the Association for the Scientific Study of Anomalous Phenomena (ASSAP). I have written ten books based on my own research, including the successful *Spontaneous Human Combustion, The Afterlife* and *The Complete Book of UFOs* with Jenny Randles. I have lectured widely and acted as consultant for major television companies.

My main purpose in writing this book has been to produce an easy-to-follow reference for car or rucksack, to enable people to visit and experience for themselves locations where strange events have been reported in the past and, in many cases, continue to be documented today. At the same time I hope the book will provide a good read on a winter's night for those who prefer to savour the eerie atmosphere of Bram Stoker's Whitby, or speculate on the true nature of the horrors of Glamis Castle, from the comfort of an armchair.

The locations selected are all accessible to the public, though obviously if your personal investigation involves a vigil on private property suitable arrangements would have to be made with the owners. To assist readers, full instructions and, in some cases, maps are included to pinpoint areas where strange events have happened. The phenomena include ghosts, poltergeists, lake and sea monsters, UFOs, vampires, witchcraft and leys.

Those keen on taking part in overnight vigils might welcome the support of a professional organization such as ASSAP, whose address is on page 213. If you have any experiences you would like to report to me, I can be contacted through my publisher. Please remember always to enclose a stamped addressed envelope if you are expecting a reply.

BE PREPARED

An investigator needs a lot of patience in order to retain his or her objectivity. Someone may witness a 'ghost', but is it really a spirit or might there be another explanation? UFO sightings are not proof of extraterrestrial spacecraft.

Phenomena do not occur to order, although there is some evidence that poltergeist activity can be triggered by certain individuals. Most of the time nothing will happen. Investigators must console themselves with recording the evidence of witnesses' testimony and looking for physical clues. Their first duty is to find a rational solution to a case.

Some basic equipment is essential. It would be foolish to visit a location where an apparition has been active, or a UFO reported on a regular basis, and be unable to record proof if something happens.

Video cameras are vital. If you only have a still camera,

remember that pocket cameras are virtually useless for outside purposes. It is no use photographing something surfacing a mile away on Llyn Tegid, for instance, if you are not using a telephoto lens. A camera loaded with daylight film (usually 100 ASA or 200 ASA) is useless for night-time shots. Even a flash gun has limitations. The investigator needs film which is more sensitive to light: 400–3,200 ASA; or infra-red film in conjunction with an infra-red emitting lamp.

CHECKLIST OF EQUIPMENT FOR INVESTIGATORS

- Video camera
- Still camera with telephoto lens
- Night-time film if appropriate
- Tape recorder
- Thermometer
- Notebook
- Pen
- Torch
- Warm Clothing
- Thermos flask
- Chalk

More Sophisticated Equipment

- Reel-to-reel sensitive stereo audio recording equipment
- Computer controlled machines for accurately measuring changes in temperature and the slight movement of objects
- Infra-red camera film with infra-red emitting lamps

Equipment should also include thermometers to record sudden drops or rises in temperature, chalk to mark the position of objects said to be moved by a poltergeist, tape recorders, notebooks and pens to record times when phenomena have occurred, and torches. Of course, if money is no object then some very sophisticated equipment can be obtained. If you are attending an all-night vigil in the grounds of a country house or on top of a windswept hill, remember to wear plenty of layers of clothing and to take a thermos flask. Even in the summer months it can turn incredibly cold during the night.

Make good use of the Tourist Information Centres listed in the book. Their staff are courteous and can provide invaluable help.

Whether you just want to read this book, drive to some of the places where strange things have happened, or carry out your own enquiries, approach this fascinating subject seriously and don't pre-judge issues. But remember that, above all, you are there to enjoy yourself.

Peter Alland

North-West England

CAUGHT BY THE OLD MAN

BEAUTY AND TRAGEDY

CONISTON is a beautiful village in the Lake District. It is the last resting place of the Victorian writer, critic and social reformer, John Ruskin, who died in 1900 and is buried in the north-east corner of the churchyard of St Andrews. Donald Campbell also died there, but he has no grave. Campbell was trying to break the world water speed record on Coniston Water in 1967 when his jet-powered Bluebird went out of control at more than 300 miles per hour. His body was never recovered. But on 15 February 1954 Coniston had become famous for a less tragic reason. That day two boys saw and photographed a 'flying saucer'; the case was to become a classic of UFO literature.

THE CONISTON SAUCER

Stephen Darbishire was the fourteen-year-old son of a local doctor. He would spend hours up near the quarries on the slopes of the Old Man of Coniston, a mountain that towers over the village, generally fooling about as boys do. That afternoon he decided to go up as usual and took with him his younger cousin, Adrian Myers. Before the boys left the house, Stephen had noted the peculiar mood of his mother, who sensed that 'something' was going to happen.

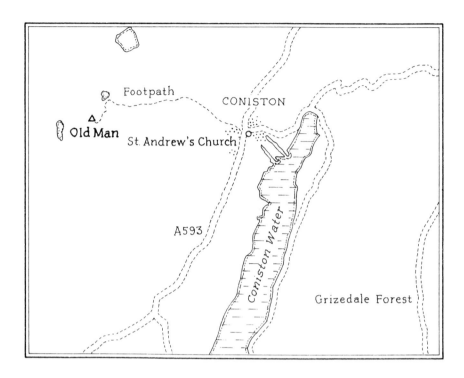

The boys were taking photographs with a Kodak camera; its focus was altered by adjusting some bellows on which the lens was mounted. Stephen thought he had set the focus on 'infinity'. Unfortunately, the bellows were not properly locked into place, so two of the most important photographs taken that day were out of focus.

At 11a.m. Adrian was looking up at the summit of the mountain and Stephen was facing the opposite direction, staring out over the gleaming surface of the lake about two miles away in the valley. Suddenly Adrian thumped his cousin on the back and shouted: 'Look at that thing!'

Stephen turned round and saw a peculiarly shaped 'cloud' moving down the slope of the Old Man. Despite its misty appearance, the object had definite shape and was completely silent. Just before it momentarily disappeared behind a rise about 100 yards away, Stephen took a picture. A few seconds later the thing reappeared and he clicked the shutter for the second and last time. The strange object then rose up and disappeared into the sky.

The boys returned home and excitedly told their parents what they had seen, but the story was met with laughter as the grown-ups thought it was just a schoolboy prank. Stephen took the film to a local chemist for processing. Afterwards, he went away for a few days to visit his godmother who lived in a neighbouring village. When he returned, it was to a homecoming he will never forget.

INTERVIEW WITH
STEPHEN DARBISHIRE

Ufologist Dr Harry Hudson and I tracked down Stephen Darbishire in 1991 and he agreed to see us. We met at a pub in Kendal, and he admitted it was the first time in twenty-five years that he had publicly discussed the matter. Stephen said: 'After speaking to you on the phone, I thought perhaps is was about time I spoke to somebody.' Commenting on his return home, he continued: 'I arrived on the early bus, and half the world's press were waiting on the doorstep. I can remember that trauma a jolly sight better than the flying saucer incident!'

Although out of focus, the two photographs showed a saucer-shaped object (see photograph 1); in the second shot there was a distortion effect down one side. The general shape was similar to photographs by American contactee George Adamski of a 'Venusian scout craft'. Using a system called 'orthographic projection', British engineer Leonard Cramp compared Darbishire's photographs with Adamski's and found both objects to be proportionally identical.

The boys were put under a lot of pressure, but they stuck to their story. Stephen later met Members of Parliament, high-ranking military officers and government scientists.

The sighting affected the entire Darbishire household, particularly his father. Dr Darbishire began building machines that he hoped would cure his patients by projecting electromagnetic radiation on to their 'auras' – invisible bands of energy which are supposed to surround the body like a halo. Stephen described his father as 'a real mad scientist'. But, according to Stephen, the

1. When schoolboy Stephen Darbishire took this photograph in 1954 in Coniston, Cumbria, it caused a stir. Scientific analysis seemed to confirm it was a similar object to one photographed by contactee George Adamski in America. Were they both hoaxed, or did Darbishire's picture confirm Adamski's story? (See pages 6–11.)

2. Chingle Hall near Goosnargh, Lancashire, was built in 1260, and in recent years has earned a strong reputation for being haunted. Many visitors have heard loud banging noises and observed apparitions. Anomalous sounds were recorded during a live BBC radio programme. (See pages 12–17.)

3. The village shop in Newchurch. Newchurch is one of several tiny villages around Pendle Hill, Lancashire, an area famous for witchcraft. In 1612 nineteen self-confessed witches, most of them from the area, were hung at Lancaster. The Hill has always had a reputation for being magical and even in this day and age local witches and Christians still vie for domination of it. (See pages 18–25.)

4. Photograph of a being which allegedly abducted a former police officer whilst he was out walking across Ilkley Moor, West Yorkshire, in December 1987. There have been several contemporary stories involving UFOs on the moor, and the area is rich in folklore. (See pages 40–47.)

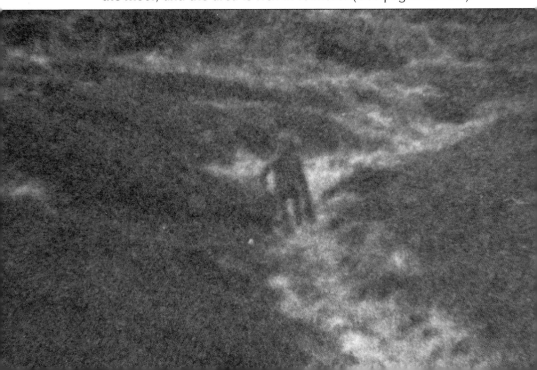

FAMOUS UFO PHOTOGRAPHS FROM ABROAD

Reports of UFOs come in from all over the world. Here are two photographic cases from abroad which bear the hallmarks of authenticity.

- Mr and Mrs Paul Trent of McMinnville, Oregon, took two daylight pictures of a disc-shaped object which flew over their farm on 11 May 1950. Expert analysis confirmed it was a large object about a mile away.
- In January 1958 Brazilian navy vessel *Almirante Saldanha* was anchored off the island of Trinidad in the South Atlantic Ocean, packed with crew and scientists involved in oceanographic studies. Many witnesses saw a saturn-shaped object flying over the island. Four photographs were taken.

---

machine did cure Donald Campbell of an illness the day before he made one of his attempts on a new world water speed record on Coniston Water.

The constant pressure of people writing, telephoning and visiting him about the incident drove Stephen to do something drastic. Naively, he thought that if he said it had all been a joke interest would wane and he could live a normal life. But then some people thought he had been 'got at by MI5' and made to deny the experience.

We found Stephen to be open-minded and sincere. He still lives in the Lake District and is a successful artist. Married, he has children of his own and is wary of protecting them from the sort of publicity that as a fourteen-year-old he had to cope with. Over lunch, he told us:

I've no idea what it was. I thought, 'there's a funny-shaped cloud.' But it wasn't a cloud. It was like something with a light inside of it, very real, and not ghostly. My father had an enquiring mind and would accept nothing. He went on for months asking me to describe it again, trying to trip me up.

It's a part of my life which happened – a one-off thing lasting about thirty seconds, just enough time to wind the camera on.

Stephen claims that the reproduction quality of the published prints is poorer than the original. But unfortunately no one can make fresh prints from the original plates, which were mysteriously stolen not long after the event.

In the 1960s members of the Aetherius Society, an international organization which has turned ufology into a religion, visited Coniston. They were on a mission to climb every mountain peak in Britain to charge them with 'prayer energy'. The Old Man of Coniston was especially chosen because of Darbishire's experience.

How to Find Coniston and the Old Man

Come off the M6 at Junction 36 and follow the A590. Turn right on to the A5084, then right on to the A593 into Coniston.

Climbing to the top of the Old Man is arduous and you should be kitted out with the right footwear. Looking south from the village centre, take the path on your right by the beck. Alternatively take a stroll on the shore of Coniston Water or wander through Grizedale Forest on the far shore: it might be safer!

See map on page 7 and also consult Ordnance Survey map 97.

NEAREST MAIN TOURIST INFORMATION CENTRE
Victoria Street, Windermere, Cumbria, LA23 1AD.
Tel: 015394 46499.

OTHER PLACES WHERE UFOS HAVE BEEN CAPTURED ON FILM

From time to time, as in the Darbishire case, UFOs are caught on film. A small number do appear to show something genuine. Building surveyor Peter Day was motoring between Thame and Aylesbury near Cuddington in Buckinghamshire when he saw something strange in the sky. It was 9 a.m. on 11 January 1973.

He stopped the car and filmed the phenomenon in the fifteen seconds before it disappeared from sight. The colour film shows a pulsating orange ball moving parallel with the tree-lined horizon. It was also witnessed by school children in Long Crendon and a teacher who was driving to work. Kodak confirmed that the image was genuine. There has been speculation that the orange ball was burning fuel ejected by an F-111 which crashed thirty miles away. However, the timing does not match and the ball did not behave like burning fuel.

The Manchester UFO Research Association (now NARO, see page 1) received an anonymous piece of daylight film dated May 1982. It showed a pulsating white ball travelling at low altitude parallel to The Solent between Gosport, near Portsmouth, and the Isle of Wight. It then did a seventy degree upward turn and disappeared into cloud. Despite pleas in the media for witnesses to come forward, MUFORA were unable to solve the mystery.

On Saturday 19 February 1994 an artist called Ian Macpherson drove to Craigluscar Reservoir, just outside Dumfermline, Fife. He took a camera with him to assist his painting, and had just begun to take photographs of the area when he heard a humming sound. Over the water he saw a disc-shaped object. For the next fifteen minutes he felt a compulsion not to take any pictures of the craft. The UFO was metallic with diffused light on its underside. As it was moving away, Ian came to his senses and took two shots.

The pictures were sent to the Ministry of Defence after being processed by the *Daily Record*. Andrew Allen, their picture editor, told paranormal investigator Malcolm Robinson that he was 'very impressed', as did Ian Torrance, the newspaper's senior photographer. The pictures are currently being analysed by the MoD.

Two days earlier, the daughter of a local farmer was bemused when the electrics on her car temporarily malfunctioned. There was no fault on the vehicle when it was checked.

There are growing numbers of unidentified flying objects being caught by *video* cameras. A small object was filmed zipping over a Wiltshire cornfield in broad daylight. The film was taken in 1991 by Steve Alexander who had been investigating a crop circle in an adjacent field when he saw the object. Just before it disappeared into the sky it also caught the attention of a nearby tractor driver. Suggestions for what the object might be have included a piece of tin foil or a puff ball from a thistle, but the small object seems to be in controlled flight.

HAUNTED CHINGLE HALL

RELIGIOUS PERSECUTION

*C*HINGLE HALL is a cross-shaped building at the end of a long, bumpy drive (see photograph 2 opposite page 8). It lies less than one mile from the Viking village of Goosnargh and five miles from Ribchester, which was the location of a Roman garrison. I can recommend the latter, having spent a leisurely afternoon in Ribchester soaking up its history.

The Hall, built in 1260 by a lesser knight called Adam de Singleton, was one of 5,300 moated manor houses built in Britain for royal owners and the Church. Chingle is one of only a hundred which survive. In 1536, when Henry VIII took control of the Church and suppressed the Catholic faith, Chingle Hall became the venue for secret masses.

Under the new regime the first execution of a priest was carried out in 1580, and more followed. Nicholas Owen, a master builder from Worcester, was secretly hired in 1600 to construct in the building several hides where fugitive priests could conceal themselves. So far six hides have been discovered – the latest as recently as 1986.

It was in 1600 that the Wall family acquired the Hall. After John Wall was baptized into the Catholic faith he went to Douai in France, where he eventually joined the Order of St Francis before returning to England. There, in the Midlands, he took up missionary work. Twenty-eight years later he was martyred in Worcester, and his friends took his head to a convent in France.

At the beginning of the French Revolution in 1789 the head was brought back to England, and is supposedly concealed in Chingle Hall. John Wall was later canonized, and it is his spirit which is thought to cause most of the manifestations around the building.

During the Battle of Preston in 1648 Oliver Cromwell reputedly came to the Hall to spy on Royalist forces from its chimney. In view of its rich history it would be surprising if Chingle Hall was *not* haunted – and haunted it undoubtedly is.

THE HAUNTING

Ghost hunter Peter Underwood has interviewed many witnesses of strange phenomena at Chingle Hall. Mrs Margaret Howarth, a former resident, told him of a plethora of poltergeist activity including door latches moving, footsteps, materialization of water and the appearance of a monk-like figure in the house and garden. She claimed that on one occasion she and her brother watched a cloaked form for fifteen minutes until it faded away.

One visitor saw two 'monks' in the act of praying, and another told Underwood he saw a figure with a pale face which was 'hardly human and surrounded by a dark cowl' peering through a window. From the first-floor Priest's Room someone witnessed a figure with shoulder-length hair walk past the window *from outside*. Numerous ghostly figures, alarming temperature drops and loud bangings have been reported by many people – and recorded too.

Guide Anna Easton told me she was 'totally convinced that the house is haunted'. She has had two sightings of an apparition, heard heavy footsteps, smelt incense and had her hair and arm stroked by an invisible presence. Anna remarked: 'I always tell visitors that some people will never experience the paranormal, but it is there at Chingle Hall for those capable of tuning in'.

One of the most persistent investigators was New Zealander Michael Bingham. While in the Priest's Room he heard a sound of bricks being moved in the opened priest's hole. He peered into it and saw a hand moving one of the bricks. The hand stopped and faded into nothing. Another researcher, Andrew Usher, was also witness to this. During his investigation, Michael also saw a cowled

---

POLTERGEISTS

The phenomena at Chingle Hall are reminiscent of the polter-geist. Poltergeists respond to people and possess intelligence. They create banging and tapping noises, cause apparitions to manifest, move objects about and generally play games. They have often been endowed with a personality. In the past the manifestations have been blamed on 'fairies' or 'boggarts' (see page 16).

In most cases the phenomenon dies out after a few months or a year or two.

See also *Epworth*, page 48, for a classic poltergeist haunting.

---

figure. He attempted to obtain objective proof of the phenomenon and showed Underwood the results, which consisted of an audio recording of heavy footsteps and ciné film of a shadowy figure.

Between May 1979 and August 1980 investigators carried out four vigils in the Priest's Room. On every occasion they experienced loud bangs which were so fierce that they caused the floor to vibrate, yet were not heard outside of the room. The sounds, sometimes accompanied with a scratching noise, travelled around the room, across the floor, up the walls and on to the ceiling. When the house manager Fred Knowles joined them, he demonstrated his ability to contact the phenomenon by rapping on a cabinet and inviting it to reply. It did so. When a recording of one such episode was played back in the room, a single rap answered the recorded request. One of the most celebrated incidents happened during a live broadcast by BBC Radio Lancashire.

THE CELEBRITY SPOOK

A 'ghost hunt' was set up by presenter Gerald Main, who invited psychic researcher Terence Whitaker and Spiritualist Colin Church to share the experience with him. It was Christmas Day 1980.

Whitaker had with him what he jokingly referred to as the 'spectre detector'. This device emitted a continuous high-pitched note, and reacted to changes in the immediate electrical field. If phenomena associated with electromagnetic energy entered the room, the equipment would warn the investigator by changing the pitch of the note.

When Colin Church joined the two men he immediately sensed the presence of a figure in a nearby bedroom. Leaving the detector behind, the team moved to the room and experienced a sudden and dramatic drop in temperature, which Colin called 'a psychic breeze'. In fact the effect is quite real, and researchers have speculated that heat energy is used by the phenomenon to make something manifest in our 'dimension'.

They brought the detector into the bedroom, and at 11p.m. the temperature dropped again. At the same time the note from the machine slowly increased in pitch. Church claimed that an entity had entered the room and was standing between them.

Things calmed down with the entrance of Fred Knowles, who started relating the story of an excavated skeleton. He was interrupted by three very distinctive loud knocks. Gerald Main asked if Knowles had banged his foot against a wooden chest, but the manager denied it.

They went back into the Priest's Room. As Knowles and Whitaker swapped stories of phantom footsteps, suddenly there were three more loud knocks. It was a few minutes to midnight. On the live programme everyone stopped talking. More bangs followed, which seemed to travel from the priest's hide out into the corridor. There was no doubt this time. All three men were standing away from the furniture. The knocks were coming from *inside* the walls.

The temperature plummeted once more, and Church felt cold air rush past him. Whitaker claimed he saw 'an indefinable shape' disappear around the back of a door. As midnight struck, Gerald Main was left trying to convince listeners that it was not a set-up and that the incidents were entirely genuine.

ALSO NEARBY – RIBCHESTER AND HOTHERSALL HALL

A Roman fort was built at Ribchester and many artefacts from that period are on display.

A footpath near the church passes by Hothersall Hall, which is situated on the north bank of the River Ribble. The Hall used to be haunted by a boggart – a spirit which can be mischievous or carry out chores for humans.

This particular boggart got out of hand and was 'laid' beneath the roots of a large laurel tree in the grounds. It is said that the boggart cannot escape as long as the tree lives. To ensure this, the roots have to be periodically fed with milk.

Ribchester is approximately five miles east of Goosnargh on the B6245.

How to Find Chingle Hall

Come off the M6 at Junction 32 and join the M55. Leave at Junction 1 and join the A6 heading north to Lancaster. After one mile turn right at Broughton on to the B5269. Goosnargh is three miles further on. Chingle Hall is on the right.

The Hall is open Easter to September, Thursday to Monday, 12 noon–4p.m. Bank Holidays and August Sundays, 10a.m.–5p.m. March and October, Sundays only, 12 noon–4p.m. There is a pleasant picnic area in an orchard near the car park.

Chingle Hall also organizes overnight vigils. *Tel: 01772 861082* for details.

Consult Ordnance Survey map 102.

NEAREST MAIN TOURIST INFORMATION CENTRE

The Guildhall, Lancaster Road, Preston, Lancashire, PR1 1HT. *Tel: 01772 253731.*

OTHER HAUNTED BUILDINGS

Why apparitions favour buildings more than the open air is a mystery. Unless the fabric of four walls is more conducive to a 'recording' of an earlier event? But how does this explain poltergeist activity, which reacts to percipients? There must be something special about buildings.

Baddesley Clinton is a medieval moated manor house dating back to 1300. It is situated at Knowle, Solihull, Warwickshire.

The house passed through the hands of three families before becoming the property of the National Trust. The Brome family who flourished at the time of Henry VI probably contributed to some of the ghostly goings-on. John Brome was killed during a dispute over a mortgage with a man called Herthill. In turn, Herthill was murdered by John's son, Nicholas. In 1485, after doing penance, Nicholas returned home to find his wife in a compromising position with the domestic chaplain. He killed the man. This happy cast of characters have been blamed for much of the phenomena in the house.

Footsteps have been repeatedly heard in deserted parts of the building, with muttered arguments in an empty room. An oppressive atmosphere in the library drove one woman out. In 1884 a lady visitor awoke in the Tapestry Room to see a fair-haired woman dressed in black disappearing through a door. Three years later the same woman slept in the State Room and saw the apparition again. Over the years both staff and guests have witnessed an identical ghost. A figure of a man has also appeared in the Red Room, and on several occasions priests' vestments have been taken from a drawer and left in a heap on the floor.

The ghosts of Gunby Hall at Burgh-le-Marsh in Lincolnshire have been linked with rumours of a double murder. Built in 1700 by Sir William Massingberd the house is set in a 1500 acre park now owned by the National Trust. Not long after it was built trouble blighted the house. According to rumour Sir William discovered that his wife, or more likely his daughter, was having an affair with one of the servants. The pair planned to run away but, before they could, Sir William shot dead the young man and dumped his body in the pond near the house. Some versions say both were murdered. Witnesses have described a sudden drop in temperature followed by the vague outline of a young couple. They have been seen on the path that runs alongside the pond which has earned the name 'The Ghost Walk'.

THE WITCHES OF PENDLE FOREST

FOCUS OF WITCHCRAFT

No PLACE IN BRITAIN has more of a reputation for witchcraft than Pendle Hill and the villages nestling around its skirt. The Forest of Pendle – a 'forest' was originally an area maintained for hunting by the monarch – is rich in tales of witchcraft both historical and present-day. In the late sixteenth century there was a war between witch families and the authorities, resulting in a famous trial at Lancaster. The hill is also the location for a holy well and supernatural visions that gave rise to a new religious order, the Quakers. Today occultists and Christian fundamentalists assemble on Pendle Hill, both claiming its power for their own.

THE PENDLE WITCHES OF 1600

The story actually began in 1595. At that time thousands of supposed witches were being arrested, tortured and executed across Europe, particularly in Germany. In England torture was illegal, although notorious official witchfinders such as Matthew Hopkins found ways around it.

The first 'supernatural' deaths around Pendle were blamed on an old woman called Chattox and her daughter Alizon, after Christopher Nutter and his son, Robert, died within a short time of one another. The women and their relatives were tenants of the Nutters on land at Higham, and had cursed the family after falling out with them.

Trouble really flared when Chattox and her family came into conflict with another family, well known for witchcraft. Old Demdike and her son-in-law John Device and his family lived at Malkin Tower near Newchurch. Local people had grumbled about these self-confessed witches for years, but it was not until 1612 that the authorities became involved.

On 18 March Alizon was travelling on the road to Trawden, just south of Colne, when she came across a pedlar called John Law. She asked him for some pins, but because she had no money, or he was just obstinate, Law refused to undo his pack. Alizon became angry and cursed him. As he turned away the man suffered a stroke. He was taken to a nearby ale-house, having lost his speech. Subsequently Abraham, his son, was sent for from Halifax. Law regained his tongue and accused Alizon of bewitchment. She admitted the charge, and Abraham had her up before a magistrate called Roger Nowell.

FURTHER CONFESSIONS

Alizon claimed that, when Law refused to give her some pins, a black dog appeared beside her which spoke in English. It offered to lame the pedlar and she gleefully accepted. Alizon went on to describe her initiation into witchcraft by her grandmother, and implicated Chattox and Demdike. Arrests followed, and 'witches' marks', were found. These were small deformities or discolourations of the skin, such as birthmarks, supposedly placed there by the Devil. Neighbours were happy to testify against the lot of them, as was Jennet Device, a nine-year-old relative of many of those accused! Demdike, Chattox and her daughter, Anne, were questioned at Ashlar House in the nearby village of Fence.

They described how the devil had appeared to them in various guises, and told of demons who aided and abetted them in killing their neighbours. One victim was a child who had been murdered using 'sympathetic magic' – a spell involving a clay doll into which pins were inserted. Altogether the women were accused of sixteen supernatural murders, plus livestock killing, graveyard robbing at Newchurch, and milk and beer souring. Bones and clay images were found at Malkin Tower.

BLACK DOGS

Black dogs are a familiar motif in folklore accounts. They are believed to be emissaries of Satan – demons in the guise of dogs. The dog is known as *Shuck* in Norfolk, *Mauthe Doog* on the Isle of Man, *Padfoot* in Staffordshire, *Cappel* in Westmoreland, *Shag Dog* in Leicestershire and *Hooter* in Warwickshire.

Sightings of black dogs – often with glowing red eyes – have been recorded in recent times around Britain and an encounter with the beast is usually an omen of death or disaster.

See also *Lower Quinton*, page 88, and *Whitby*, page 34, for further incidents involving black dogs.

On Good Friday in 1612 some twenty witches met at Malkin Tower to plot the release of those already arrested. Amongst these was Alice Nutter (no direct relation of Christopher and Robert Nutter), a participant of high social standing, who lived at Roughlee Old Hall. But Nowell heard of the gathering and more arrests ensued.

On 19 August they were put on trial at Lancaster Assizes before a jury and found guilty. Nineteen men and women, mostly from the Pendle area, died on the gallows.

In 1633 seventeen people were accused of witchcraft in Hoarstones, a hamlet near the village of Fence, and condemned to death. Fortunately they were reprieved by the King after a hoax was discovered.

PENDLE HILL

The Big End of Pendle Hill marks it for miles around: the sheer drop looms out of nowhere and can be seen by travellers on distant motorways. A pile of stones on the Big End marks a Bronze Age burial. For centuries the hill was used as a signalling station,

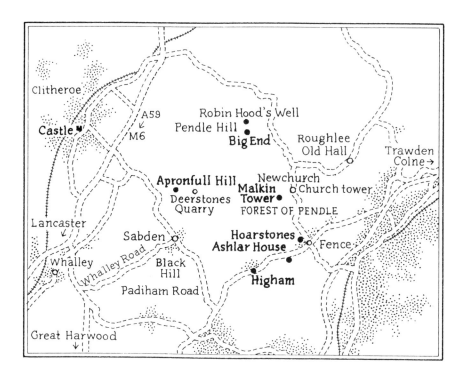

initially to warn of Scottish invaders. A beacon was last lit there in 1887 to commemorate Queen Victoria's Jubilee.

One does not need a specialist knowledge of the area to realize that the hill harbours something above the ordinary. It is awesome and magical, and draws those who would make use of its indefatigable power. The hill forges a link between our eggshell-thin 'civilization' and a more basic, ancient authority.

A subsidiary tor on its western slope is called Apronfull Hill. Legend recalls how a giant named Owd Nick stood here after striding over from Deerstones Quarry – leaving his footprints behind in the stones. On the hill he took a boulder from his apron and threw it at Clitheroe Castle, making a gaping hole. The effort caused the strings of his apron to break and the remaining boulders fell to the ground – where they can still be seen.

In 1646 George Fox climbed to the summit and surveyed the villages below. There he received a vision from God and started the Quaker movement, known today as the Society of Friends.

PENDLE FOREST AND THE NEW WITCH HUNT

In the late 1980s a new witch hunt came to Britain from the USA. Christian fundamentalists and social workers were claiming that children were abused and even sacrificed by occultists in the name of Satan. Dozens of children were taken from their homes across the country by the authorities, who believed they were at risk from parents and family friends immersed in Satanism. The term 'satanic ritual abuse' was coined. By 1993 the whole thing had fizzled out after the fundamentalists had been unable to produce one shred of evidence.

In 1989 I was working on a book which was partly an investigation into these claims. My research took me to Sabden at the foot of Pendle Hill, where a white witch named Yvonne Foley gave me an interview. I reached Sabden over Black Hill along Padiham Road, which twists and climbs before plummeting towards the miniature houses below.

MODERN WITCHES

According to a firm which supplies witchcraft paraphernalia, there are around 25,000 witches in Britain. Their pagan religion is based on worshipping the Earth Mother and other nature gods and goddesses. Most claim to be white witches who use their powers for good, such as healing. Because of bad publicity, however, covens meet at secret locations to practise their rituals and carry out ceremonies.

See *Lower Quinton*, page 88, for a tale of witchcraft murder.

Yvonne was blue-eyed and blonde and very charming. While decrying the new witch hunt, she made it clear that witchcraft, in its Earth Mother guise, was alive and well and thriving in Pendle. After she moved to Sabden, the established witches had gone out of their way to make her comfortable.

A few miles south of Sabden, off the A666 (the sign of the Beast as described in Revelation 13) in Great Harwood, lives the vicar of

St John's, the Revd Kevin Logan. One of the main witchfinders during that time, he took part in countless television and radio programmes and was widely featured in the press. When I spoke to him he claimed to know of thirty covens operating in the area.

The Revd Logan was convinced of the threat of Satanism around Pendle and the power of the hill. To counter its 'misuse', local churches had wanted to erect a 20-foot-high rolled-steel cross on Big End, but the council would not grant planning permission.

Places to Visit in Pendle Forest

Pilgrims flock to the summit of Pendle Hill on two dates. The first is Good Friday, on which a Christian service was reintroduced in 1985, and the second is the night of 31 October – Halloween. The latter event is attended by curiosity seekers and local covens initiating new members.

To the east of Big End is Robin Hood's Well, named after a Celtic character called Robin Goodfellow. It is a pagan spring which became a holy well when Christians turned their attention to it. Visitors who want to climb to the summit of Pendle Hill must be in reasonably fit condition and wear sensible hill-walking footwear.

The quaint village of Newchurch boasts a church tower dating from 1712. Set into it is an oval piece of glass called the Eye of God, which was placed there to watch over the unrighteous. It must be disapproving of the village shop, which sells witchcraft paraphernalia (see photograph 3 opposite page 9)! In St Mary's churchyard is a tombstone known as the 'witch's grave'. Although adorned with a skull and crossbones and bearing the name of 'Nutter', who lies there is unknown. It is not, however, the resting place of Alice from Roughlee Old Hall. On the edge of Newchurch is Malkin Tower, thought to be the meeting place of the witches.

Roughlee Old Hall – the 'Witches Hall' – built by Miles Nutter in 1536, still stands in Roughlee, although it has been extensively altered.

NEARBY - LANCASTER PRISON

Lancaster Prison is where the Lancashire witches were held and executed. From Pendle take the A671 to Whalley, then the A59 to Junction 31 of the M6. Lancaster is 25 miles north of this junction.

The prison is housed in a castle built on the site of previous forts, the first dating from AD 79 and built by the Romans. At the moment it is still a working prison, but is due for closure at the end of the century. Parts of the castle are progressively being opened to the public.

From Castle Hill you can see the Witches' (or Well) Tower. This originated in the early 1200s, but was rebuilt around 1500. Beneath the tower are three dungeons where the Pendle witches were held in freezing, airless conditions. An exhibition about the prison can be viewed at the Tourist Information Centre at 29 Castle Hill. *Tel: 0524 32878*.

How to Find the Forest of Pendle

Come off the M6 at Junction 31 and join the A677. Less than two miles later turn left on to the A59 to Whalley. You are now on the edge of the 'forest', and need to consult a detailed map to decide where to visit first. Whalley Road, which leads directly to Sabden, is a good place to start.

See map on page 21 and also consult Ordnance Survey map 103.

NEAREST MAIN TOURIST INFORMATION CENTRE
12–14 Market Place, Clitheroe, Lancashire BB7 2DA.
Tel: 01200 25566.

OTHER PLACES ASSOCIATED WITH WITCH HUNTS

Manningtree in Essex was the home of the Witchfinder General Matthew Hopkins, who carved out quite a successful career for himself between 1644 and 1646. A lawyer by training, he managed to get four 'witches' hung after convincing the court they

5. The prehistoric Rollright Stones, near Lower Quinton in Warwickshire. It is said that they represent a king and his men who were turned into stone by a witch. She, in turn, was changed into an elder tree. Modern covens meet at the circle under cover of darkness. (See pages 88–94.)

6. Glastonbury Tor, Somerset, is crowned by the ruins of St Michael's Church. The town of Glastonbury features heavily in Arthurian legend, while the Tor is the location for contemporary UFO sightings. (See pages 110–117.)

7. Chalice Well, situated at the foot of the Tor, is supposed to possess magical powers. (See page 114.)

had sent a demon to murder him in the garden of his house. Subsequently local authorities paid him to seek out witches.

Hopkins and his henchmen walked the fine line between psychological and physical pressure, and the illegal torture of suspects. Such was the fear his presence generated that people would fall at his feet confessing without pressure being applied at all. Hundreds were imprisoned at his behest, and two hundred were hung before he fell from glory.

South of the village of St John's, on the Isle of Man, is the hill of Slieu Whallian. Here witches were punished by being rolled downhill in barrels full of spikes. It is supposedly haunted by the screams of a murdered witch, heard amid howling winds.

The witch hunts rampaged across Europe, Britain and later parts of America. Thousands, possibly up to a million alleged witches comprising men, women and children, were tortured and put to death in horrifying ways. Many witches were burnt at St Andrews in Lothian, Strathclyde in the sixteenth and seventeenth centuries. These executions were carried out on Witch Hill to the west of the city and on Methven's Tower which survives as part of the ruins of St Andrews Cathedral.

Near Dunning, to the west of St Andrews, on the B8062 travelling to Auchterarder, is a stone memorial to Maggie Wall, a witch burned in 1657. At Dornoch, just off the A9 north of Inverness, in a garden near the golf course, is a rough bluish stone that marks the spot where Janet Horne was burnt to death in 1772. She was the last witch to be executed in Scotland.

THE EDGE OF THE SUPERNATURAL

A BEAUTY SPOT RICH IN LEGEND

THERE ARE MANY PLACES in Britain associated with the legend of King Arthur (see also pages 110–117). The Edge at Alderley has strong connections with Merlin, and a tradition of witchcraft past and present.

The village of Alderley was originally called Chorley. When the Birmingham Railway Company built a station there in the mid-nineteenth century they called it 'Alderley and Chorley'. Then it was decided to change the name altogether, because it caused confusion with other places called Chorley in the north of England. The sandstone escarpment rising east of the station was called 'The Edge', so around 1850 the village officially became 'Alderley Edge'.

The Edge itself offers woodland walks, caves, a holy well and breathtaking views. It rises 600 feet above sea level and is about two miles long. The escarpment commands a panorama over Macclesfield, the Peak District National Park and the 1,091 foot summit of Mow Cop. In 1947 both the Edge and Wizard Wood were handed over to the National Trust.

The discovery of primitive artefacts suggests that man occupied the caves around six thousand years ago. Stone hammers, now on view in Manchester Museum, indicate that copper was mined in shallow workings before Roman times. The area has been designated one of Special Scientific Interest.

HOLY WELLS

There are hundreds of Holy Wells in Britain which were once part of a water cult invested with gods. They were considered 'sacred' thousands of years before Christianity adopted them.

Many wells are said to have sprung out of the earth in response to an event such as the death of a king during battle, as illustrated by St Oswald's Well at Winwick, Cheshire. Others were thought to have magical healing effects such as Coed y Ffynnon at Penmachno, Caernarfon.

Ghosts are also associated with a lot of wells including The Well of the Spectre at Dunlichty, Inverness, and the Three Tree Well near Glasgow.

It is a centre of antiquity, paganism, legend and modern supernatural experience. Alan Garner set his occult children's novel *The Weirdstone of Brisingamen*, which was later filmed for television, at the Edge.

THE WIZARD OF EDGE

There is a story of a farmer travelling three hundred years ago from Mobberley to Macclesfield, where he intended to sell a white mare at the market. On the Edge he was approached by a wizard who offered to buy the horse from him, but the farmer thought it would fetch a better price in Macclesfield.

He continued his journey but discovered he was unable to sell it at the market. On his return he was once more approached by the wizard, who again offered to buy the mare. The stranger led him through the woods towards the rock face. When he touched it, the rock was transformed into a pair of iron gates. The farmer followed the wizard inside a cavern filled with gold and a company of sleeping men and horses.

The wizard explained that these were King Arthur and his knights, sleeping until a time when England was in dire need of them, when they would awaken and come to the country's rescue. But they were one horse short, and that was why the wizard,

---

ARTHURIAN LEGENDS

The legend of King Arthur comes from a period of history that is largely undocumented, so it is not possible to say with certainty that Arthur existed. The story was popularised by Sir Thomas Malory in his book *Morte d'Arthur* (1485). Malory drew on sources from several European countries where the legend was recorded and the story centres around Arthur, who was predestined to become king of the Britons when he drew a sword embedded in a stone. Other components of the story include a round table, the castle of Camelot and a love tryst involving Arthur's wife, Queen Guenevere.

See also *Glastonbury*, page 110, which plays an important role in the legend.

---

whom we know as Merlin, wanted to buy the farmer's mare.

The man took the gold he was now offered and made his escape. As he left the mouth of the cavern, the gates crashed behind him and disappeared into the rock face once more. The gates have supposedly been seen again, by a maidservant.

Along the woodland path to Castle Rock is a wishing well known as the Wizard's Well, which is said to promote fertility. Follow the main path from the B5087 until another path branches

The Wizard's Well

off at right-angles. Turn left here and follow the path past rocky outcrops to the well. Above it, carved into the rock, is an inscription which reads:

> *Drink of this and take thy fill*
> *For the water falls by the wizard's will*

THE WILD MAN OF THE WOODS

Are modern sightings of a naked bearded man that of the Welsh magician Merlin?

Visitors to the woods have caught sight of a strange figure who appears to be both flesh-and-blood and supernatural. A little girl who had wandered from her parents suddenly ran back to them exclaiming that she had seen a naked man with a long beard in the trees. A courting couple were surprised by a similar figure who appeared out of the undergrowth before them, then disappeared while they watched. A retired police officer and his wife were enjoying a picnic on the Edge when they became aware of being watched from some bushes. Years of police training prepared the former officer for the situation. He calmly stood up and set off in the opposite direction, then circled round and saw a short, long-haired man. Stealthily he crept nearer and nearer, and then, when he was just a few yards away, the naked man vanished.

WITCHCRAFT

The Edge has long been thought of as a centre for supernatural power. According to one prominent Manchester witch, covens operated there during the witch hunts of the sixteenth century and continue to do so today. She told me that at certain times of the year secret meetings are held amongst the trees to celebrate the old pagan gods and goddesses such as Pan, Diana and Ishtar.

Halloween celebrations at the Edge have got out of hand in recent years. The celebration was attracting hundreds of sightseers, and police were worried that in the darkness people would fall over the escarpment. In 1993, officers blockaded the road and turned people away.

How to Find Alderley Edge

The village is just a few miles south of Manchester on the A34. Access to the Edge is off the B5087, from where it is signposted. There is a large car park nearby.

Consult Ordnance Survey map 118.

NEAREST MAIN TOURIST INFORMATION CENTRE
Town Hall Extension, Lloyd Street, Manchester, M60 2LA. *Tel: 0161 234 3157/3158.*

OTHER PLACES ASSOCIATED WITH THE LEGEND OF KING ARTHUR

Apart from Alderley Edge and Glastonbury there are many other places associated with the Arthurian legend, although it is not possible to detail them all.

Geoffrey of Monmouth placed Arthur's birth in Tintagel Castle, Cornwall. The ruins, set on a cliff, offer an amazing view. On the shore below is Merlin's Cave. The wizard assisted in the conception of Arthur using his magic.

When the coast at Zennor was invaded by the Danes, it was supposedly Arthur who defeated them near Pendeen.

Dozmary Pool on Bodmin Moor, close to the road between St Neot and Bolventor, is allegedly the lake where Sir Bedivere tossed away Excalibur as Arthur lay dying.

King Arthur defeated the Saxons near Shapwick in Dorset. The battle was fought at Badbury Rings, a hill identified in the legend as Mount Badon. The Iron Age hill fort still survives in part and can be reached by a footpath off the B3082. A golden coffin is said to be buried at the site.

Sir Thomas Malory, in *Morte d'Arthur*, located the round table at Winchester in Hampshire. The thirteenth-century Castle Hall near Westgate houses a table divided into twenty-five places. Although it is very old and of historic interest, experts feel it is unlikely to have been the famous table.

At Brent Knoll in Somerset is an isolated hill crowned with the remains of an Iron Age fort, eight miles south of Weston-Super-

Mare off the B3140. In legend it was the Mount of Frogs where the three giants slain by Sir Ider lived. In the same county lies Cadbury Castle, another Iron Age fort dating to around the time of Arthur. This is the favourite location for Camelot, and ghostly riders have been heard travelling along nearby Arthur's Lane.

King Arthur's Cave lies in a wood on the north bank of the River Wye at Whitchurch just inside the border of Hereford and Worcester. The bones of mammoths and woolly rhinoceroses have been excavated from inside. According to folklore when Arthur was on the run he hid in the cave and buried treasure there, protected from discovery by a spell from Merlin.

Wales is rich in Arthurian lore especially as Merlin was supposedly born in Carmarthen during the sixth century. The wizard is said to lie sleeping in a cave inside Merlin's Hill, situated three miles east of the town on the A40.

St Govan's Chapel at Botherston in Dyfed dates from the thirteenth century, although another existed there as early as the fifth. There is no record of a St Govan, so the name is probably a corruption of 'Gowain', one of Arthur's knights. Sir Gowain is said to have hidden from his enemies inside a cleft of rock in the chapel which closed around him. Tradition has it that he was buried beneath the altar. The tiny chapel is reached down a flight of steps cut into giant rocks that all but swallow it.

North-East England

THE LAIR OF COUNT DRACULA

THE ARRIVAL OF EVIL

One of the greatest and suddenest storms on record has just been experienced here, with results both strange and unique. The only sail noticeable was a foreign schooner with all sails set. Shortly before ten o'clock the stillness of the air grew quite oppressive. A little after midnight came a strange sound from over the sea, and high overhead the air began to carry a strange, faint, hollow booming. Then without warning the tempest broke.

On the summit of East Cliff the new searchlight was ready. Before long it discovered some distance away a schooner, apparently the same vessel which had been noticed earlier. The wind had by this time backed to the east, and there was a shudder amongst the watchers on the cliff as they realised the terrible danger in which she now was.

The searchlight followed her, and a shudder ran through all who saw her, for lashed to the helm was a corpse, with drooping head, which swung horribly to and fro at each motion of the ship. A great awe came on all as they realised that the ship, as if by a miracle, had found the harbour, unsteered save by the hand of a dead man!

But, strangest of all, the very instance the shore was touched, an immense dog sprang up on deck from below, and running forward, jumped from the bow on to the sand. Making straight for the steep cliff, where the churchyard hangs over the laneway to the East Pier, it disappeared in the darkness.

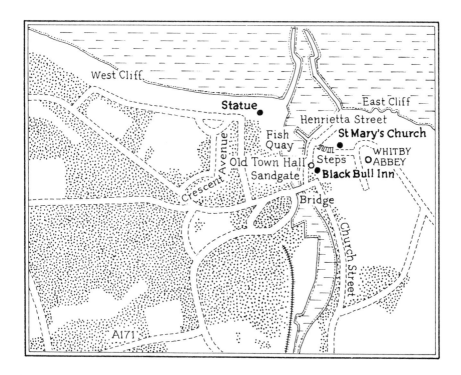

THIS IS HOW the fictitious newspaper the *Dailygraph* reported the coming of Count Dracula to Whitby in Bram Stoker's classic novel. The vampire had left his castle in Transylvania intent on building an empire of evil in England, and his arrival on the Russian schooner *Demeter* disguised as a black dog was to bring horror to the picturesque small fishing town. Holidaymakers Mina Murray and her friend Lucy Westenra in particular were to feel the blood lust attentions of the Count.

Whitby's charming old-fashioned shops and red-roofed houses spread out behind the harbour mouth, flanked by majestic cliffs. At the top of the East Cliff are two man-made features that dominate the old port. One is the ruined Abbey which is visible for miles inland and out at sea. The first monastery was built on the site in AD 657 under the instructions of Hilde, niece of Oswy, King of Northumbria. The present Abbey survived until its dissolution in 1539. Its stark stone arches stand out in relief against the sky like the perfect backdrop for a gothic horror film.

DRACULA LOCATIONS

Next to the Abbey, perched on the clifftop overlooking the town, is St Mary's parish church with its old graveyard. This was the location for several scenes in Bram Stoker's novel. The church is reached by climbing 199 steps, and it was up these that the coffin of the *Demeter*'s Russian captain was carried. The graveyard was the favourite place of Lucy and Mina, who would sit on a bench resting on the tombstone of a suicide. It was on this bench that the body of Swales, an old whaler, was discovered – Dracula's first victim in Whitby.

Later, after the funeral, Mina was to awake to find her friend gone. From the West Cliff she saw Lucy sitting on the churchyard bench with a dark figure bending over her. Mina ran down the steep steps, along Fish Quay, over the bridge and up the 199 steps to the church. She called out to Lucy and the menacing figure straightened up. 'There was undoubtedly something, long and black, bending over the half reclining white figure. I called in fright, "Lucy! Lucy!" and something raised a head, and from where I was I could see a white face and red, gleaming eyes'. Alas, despite the attempts of Mina, Jonathan Harker and Dr Van Helsing, Lucy becomes a vampire and is released from her bondage only when a stake is hammered through her heart.

VAMPIRES

The vampire has its origins in Transylvania. Vlad Tepes 'The Impaler', or Prince Dracula as he was more commonly known, was a fifteenth-century soldier who tortured to death over 100,000 people using wooden stakes. Belief was also fuelled in the seventeenth-century by Elizabeth Bathory, a Transylvanian Countess who bathed in the blood of young girls to preserve her youth. Before the advent of modern resuscitation techniques, people were sometimes buried alive and the sound of them scratching the inside of the coffin lid further encouraged the belief in the 'undead'. In fact until 1823 people who had committed suicide were often impaled with a wooden stake to stop them rising from the grave.

Bram Stoker cleverly wove into the story other features connected with the town. During his trips to Whitby the author stayed at 7 Royal Crescent – later changed to Crescent Avenue. In the book Samuel Billington is said to live at 7 The Crescent. Stoker's landlady was Fanny Harker. Jonathan Harker was one of the main characters in the story.

LOCAL LEGENDS

Stoker was probably aware of local legends, and several of these seem to have found their way into *Dracula*. One of them refers to the 'barguest', a demon which could shape-shift into the form of a monstrous black hound (see page 20). It haunted the night-time streets with its burning red eyes. Those who heard it shriek or roar were doubly afraid because they knew they were about to die.

When St Mary's graveyard was in use it attracted the attentions of a ghostly visitor. The remains of many mariners lie beneath the crooked, overgrown gravestones. Sometimes, on the night after the burial of a seaman, a coach pulled by six black horses would appear on Green Lane between the church and the Abbey. It was illuminated with torches held by two outriders, and driven by a ghostly coachman. All three were dressed in black.

The coach would shudder to a halt by the freshly dug grave. A door would open and out would step a procession of mourners who surrounded the grave. Then the dead seaman would rise up from the ground and return with the mourners into the coach. It would then rattle and bang down the church steps and turn right into Henrietta Street, then over the cliff into the foaming sea. It was thought that the spirit of the sea had sent the coach to reclaim souls which she thought were rightly hers.

MODERN GHOST STORIES

One story that Stoker could not have known about occurred in the 1950s. In those days the local railway company still employed a 'knocker-upper' to wake up staff on the early morning shift by tapping on their bedroom windows with a long pole. One morning he was on the East Side, walking between the old Town Hall and the Black Bull Inn and about to turn into Church Street, when suddenly, from around the corner of the Black Bull, there appeared a man in a swirling black cape. A collision was inevitable, yet the figure did not swerve but carried on relentlessly. It walked *right through* the knocker-upper, who fell to the ground. The apparition, cape still streaming behind him, carried on into Sandgate.

On the West Cliff stands a statue to the famous explorer Captain Cook, a Whitby man. From the beach below, several witnesses have observed a strange phenomenon emanating from the cliff face. An old man told local historian Paul McDermott of his experience around 1907. He was with a number of boy scouts who had built a camp fire on the beach when suddenly their attention was drawn to the cliff just beneath the memorial. 'As we looked up, we saw a white, misty figure – you couldn't tell if it was a man or a woman – floating down the face of the cliff. We ran over to the spot where we thought it would land, but it disappeared the instant before it reached the sand.'

The old man observed that there was no fog or mist about that evening. Another witness, seventy-five years later, saw the same phenomenon. She and her husband, on holiday in Whitby, were on the beach with their dog. As they passed beneath the statue she saw a wraith-like form appear, which floated down the cliff face and disappeared before reaching the ground. The woman was stupefied, and looked around for her husband. But he had taken off, and refused to discuss the matter.

How to Find Whitby

From York take the A64 to Scarborough, then the A171 into Whitby. Alternatively, at Malton on the A64 turn north on to the A169. This route is slightly shorter and goes right through the North Yorkshire Moors. At the junction with the A171, turn right.

See map on page 35 and also consult Ordnance Survey map 94.

NEAREST MAIN TOURIST INFORMATION CENTRE
Langborne Road, Whitby, North Yorkshire, YO21 1YN.
Tel: 01947 602674.

OTHER PLACES FEATURED IN HORROR STORIES

That other classic horror story, *Dr Jekyll and Mr Hyde* by Robert Louis Stevenson, also makes use of actual locations. The story explores the dark side that exists in us all. Through the use of a potion, Dr Jekyll's alter ego, Mr Hyde, takes complete control, even transforming his body into something loathesome and ugly. What starts as a scientific experiment gets out of control when Hyde seeks to become the dominant personality and bury the good doctor forever. Setting out from his rented rooms in Soho, Hyde stalks the streets of London committing terrible acts of cruelty and murder.

It is in Regent's Park that, without warning, the doctor changes into the hideous monster. From there he catches a hansom cab to a hotel in Portland Street and writes a letter to his friend, Dr Hastie. In his house in Cavendish Square, Dr Lanyon watches the remarkable transformation of Hyde back into the respectable Dr Jekyll.

Contemporary practitioners of the craft have also set their supernatural tales in our towns and cities, to good effect. Two of the most successful writers in this field are Ramsey Campbell and Clive Barker who have broken with tradition, abandoning haunted manor houses and dark sinister woods for the modern-day back streets of Liverpool. Campbell and Barker successfully juxtapose the nitty gritty of life in this city with intrusions from 'other worlds'. Clive Barker's bestseller *Weaveworld* tells the story of a race of beings pursued across time by their evil enemies. The beings evade capture by being encoded into the weave of a carpet, stored in a house in Liverpool.

ENCOUNTERS ON ILKLEY MOOR

A LITTLE GREEN MAN

ON 1 DECEMBER 1987 former police officer Philip Spencer set off from his home in Ilkley at 7.10a.m. He intended crossing the moor to visit a relative in the village of East Morton. Philip had only lived in the town for a short while, so as an experienced walker he took with him a compass in case the weather turned nasty. He also carried a camera to photograph Ilkley from the moors as day broke on that winter morning.

After saying goodbye to his wife and children, he set off along a footpath which took him past the old spa known as the White Wells building, then up a hill towards a stand of trees. As he walked by the opening to an old excavation in the hill top, something caught his attention. He turned, and was shocked by what he saw.

Just ten feet away from him stood 'a small green creature'. It turned and ran further into the hollow, then stopped again. Philip shouted and brought the camera up to his eye. The thing was facing him and making a dismissive motion with its right arm. The camera shutter clicked.

After taking the picture he ran down into the pit towards the creature, which disappeared behind an outcrop. Philip turned the corner – where another surprise awaited him. The creature had gone, but there before him hovered a silver, saucer-shaped craft. Before he had time to react, it shot up into the sky.

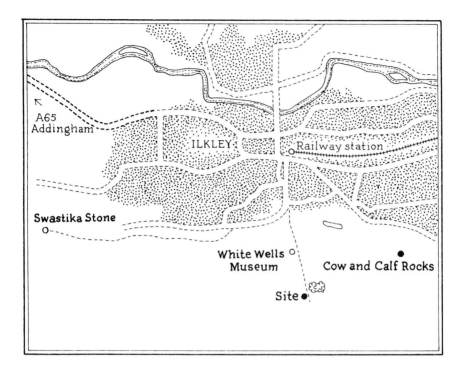

Philip was bemused. Instead of continuing the journey he went back into Ilkley. By his estimation it should have been around 8.15, but the streets were alive with shoppers, and when he looked at the church clock he saw it was 10a.m. Almost two hours had gone from his life.

He wondered if he had imagined the whole thing, but then he remembered taking the photograph. There was a film processor's in nearby Keighley who did a one-hour service. Philip caught a bus and had the film developed. On exposure 10 was the picture. It was not the best photograph in the world, but there was no mistaking the creature he had seen on the moor. . . . (See photograph 4 opposite page 9).

THE INVESTIGATION

When I first heard of the case I thought it had to be a hoax. It sounded unbelievable and the picture left me with mixed feelings.

According to Philip it had been taken without thought or time to adjust the speed and aperture setting – consequently it was under-exposed and there was a degree of camera shake. That explanation was fair enough, but alternatively a hoaxer might produce a similar picture to disguise what might be a dummy.

During my first interview I put the hoax hypothesis to him. Philip just shrugged his shoulders and said: 'I don't see the point of that. I've got better things to do with my time.' Certainly none of the usual reasons for a fraud was evident. Philip was adamant that his true identity must never be divulged. 'It would ruin me socially and professionally,' he said. So he did not want his name in lights, nor was he interested in the money that tabloid newspapers would have paid for rights to the photograph and his story.

A psychological examination found no evidence of psychosis. The only option left was that Philip was a front man for a team out to discredit investigators once the story had become established as a 'classic case'. At the time of writing this does not appear to be the explanation.

UFO ABDUCTIONS

UFO abductions are a global cross-cultural phenomenon. Before the industrial revolution abductions were perceived in the context of encounters with 'fairy folk'.

Abduction experiences present a dichotomy for experts who argue whether they are subjective or objective. They appear to be both: an objective phenomenon which affects individuals in a subjective way.

About a week after the experience, Philip noticed that his compass was altered: its polarity had been reversed, so that it now pointed south. I set up a scientific investigation of the case. The compass was examined at UMIST (University of Manchester Institute of Science and Technology), where it was discovered that ordinary magnets available to the public had no permanent effect on a similar compass. Only very powerful industrial magnets available in Japan or a rapidly applied or 'pulsed' magnetic field generated by mains electricity could alter the polarity. Did Philip possess the necessary technical knowledge, or was the compass affected by an electromagnetic field associated with the UFO?

The negative of the picture was examined by Kodak. All they could say with certainty was that it had not been tampered with. What was in the picture had actually been on the moor. Measurements confirmed that the figure – whatever it turned out to be – stood approximately four feet six inches tall.

The Radiological Protection Service loaned me one of their staff to go up to Ilkley and test for abnormal levels of radiation. Some close encounter witnesses have exhibited the symptoms of radiation poisoning. In this instance only normal background radiation was found.

HYPNOTIC REGRESSION

As the investigation proceeded, Philip grew more concerned about the missing time. Finally we arranged for hypnotic regression to be carried out by a clinical psychologist. Hypnosis is used extensively by psychoanalysts. During this state of altered consciousness, the subject is taken back to 're-live' an incident that has caused trauma. However, hypnosis is not like a truth drug.

Under hypnosis, Philip described leaving home, then – before reaching the top of the hill – how the entity first approached him, sent him into paralysis and took him inside the saucer-shaped craft. There he was examined on a table by several of the creatures, and afterwards given a conducted tour of the ship. While still under hypnosis, he was asked for a detailed description of one of the beings: 'It's quite small. He's got big pointed ears and big eyes. They're quite dark. He hasn't got a nose. He's only got a little mouth. And his hands are enormous. And his arms are long. He's got funny feet. They're like a V shape, like two big toes. He shuffles rather than walks. It's got three big fingers, like sausages. Big sausages.'

After the beings had finished with him blackness descended, and he was back on the moor, walking up the path. From this point on Philip had no conscious memory, even under hypnosis, of the events just described. The 'abduction' memory was edited out. Then he suddenly sees the creature, the surprise evident, as he raises his camera and takes a picture. . . .

Is the case genuine, or did Philip Spencer drag a four-and-a-half-foot dummy up on to the moor and then photograph it? There does not seem to be any reason why he should have done so. Jim Singleton, the clinical psychologist who examined Philip and carried out the hypnosis, believes the subject was recounting a genuine experience. Philip's reactions compared well with his clinical patients who had suffered more down-to-earth traumas, such as car accidents.

The pit where Philip took his picture is the ideal location for a UFO encounter. Who excavated the hilltop, and why? My enquiries with local historians threw no light on the matter, which seems to indicate that the work was not done in recent times. One man speculated it might be an iron ore pit from the Bronze Age. Or did something from outer space hit the hilltop and create the crater-like depression?

OTHER ENCOUNTERS

Whatever the truth of Philip Spencer's story, it is not on its own. According to a local investigator, three walkers lost some time after a ball of light hovered above them, afterwards guiding them off the moor. The Cow and Calf Rocks, just a quarter of a mile from the site of Philip Spencer's experience, have been the location for various light phenomena, including columns of light. Researcher Paul Devereux believes these are a natural energy source generated by seismic stress.

There is a reliable rumour that a serving police officer also suffered a UFO abduction on the moor. He was on duty at the time and up on the Cow and Calf Rocks.

A woman recently contacted me about her unusual sighting. At the time, in summer 1987, she and her husband lived in Ilkley. They were returning home between 1 and 2a.m. along the Addingham road when they saw a mass of white lights hovering over the rocks. The woman's initial thought was that they were the lights from a farmhouse – until she realized there were no buildings on that part of the moor. They observed the phenomenon all the way into Ilkley. She told me: 'To this day we regret

EARTH LIGHT PHENOMENA

Researcher Paul Devereux coined the term 'earth light' in 1980. He and other researchers, such as Michael Persinger, discovered that light phenomena occurred over fault lines. Scientists had already noted that lights were seen in areas prone to earthquake activity.

Can rock put under pressure beneath the earth's crust release electrical discharges into the atmosphere? Devereux speculated that this phenomenon might interface with the brain of an observer, causing them to induce a UFO experience.

See also *Barmouth*, page 198, which is a good example of light phenomena.

doing nothing about it. We lived just two minutes' drive away from the Cow and Calf Rocks, yet we just parked and went inside'.

The moor is steeped in a weird history. Not far from the UFO site is a swastika stone – the ancient sign for good, whose direction the Nazis reversed, making it a symbol for power and evil. The White Wells building was constructed around a natural spring and bequeathed to the people of Ilkley by a wealthy landowner at the beginning of the nineteenth century. William Butterfield, the bathman, witnessed a strange sight when he went to unlock the premises one morning in 1815:

> . . . all over the water and dipping into it was a lot of little creatures dressed in green, none of them more than eighteen inches high, and making a chatter and a jabber. They seemed to be taking a bath, only they bathed with all their clothes on. Then away the whole tribe went, helter skelter, toppling and tumbling, heads over heels, heels over heads, and all the while making a noise.

The green creatures made off up towards the hill where Philip Spencer was to have his experience 162 years later. What connection could there be between them? Remember Philip's description of the entities' feet: 'they're like a V shape, like two big toes.' What was an 'extraterrestrial' doing with cloven feet?

HOW TO FIND ILKLEY MOOR AND THE ENTITY LOCATION

Come off the M62 at Junction 26 and take the M606 signposted to Bradford. After two miles turn left on to the A6177 ring road, then follow the A650 to Keighley. Three miles past Keighley turn right on to the A6034 for five miles to Addingham. At Addingham turn right on to the A65 for six miles into Ilkley.

In Ilkley town centre, just before the railway station, is a sign to the moor. There is plenty of room to park. Take the path that runs to the left of the White Wells building, which is visible from the road. This is now a museum and well worth a look. The next leg of the short journey is very steep.

Follow the path behind the museum up into a gully. Take the path to the right up the side of the hill. The stand of trees on the left is where Philip Spencer was paralysed by the entity. Continue for about 100 yards up the path to the crown of the hill. On your right is the pit where Spencer photographed the being. Walk into the pit and around the outcropping, where there is an even deeper excavation about 40 feet across. This is where the silver disc hovered.

See map on page 41 and also consult Ordnance Survey map 104.

NEAREST MAIN TOURIST INFORMATION CENTRE
Station Road, Ilkley, West Yorkshire. *Tel: 01943 602319.*

OTHER SCENES OF UFO ABDUCTIONS

Just thirty-five miles south of Ilkley on the A646 lies Todmorden. The town was the location for another UFO abduction experience, also involving a police officer!

PC Alan Godfrey was on patrol car duty in the early morning of 28 November 1980. At 5 a.m. he was driving north west along Burnley Road, planning to turn right into Furney Lee Road. Instead, something up ahead caught his attention and he drove straight on. It looked like a bus slewed across the road with all its lights ablaze. As he drew nearer Godfrey saw he was mistaken. Straddling the road was an object shaped like a spinning top. He stopped the car, headlights bouncing off the UFO's metallic surface.

Suddenly, the object was gone, and the police car was several hundred yards further up Burnley Road. Godfrey was confused, and drove back to the police station where another officer agreed to return with him to examine the road. Even though it had been raining, the surface was dry where the object had been hovering.

There was a period of around twenty minutes, from the moment he stopped the car to its relocation further up the road, which was 'missing'. Hypnotic regression produced a scenario in which Godfrey found himself inside a room being examined by small beings …

It is more unusual for a group of people to suffer an abduction, but this apparently happened to three adults and two children on the evening of 19 June 1978. They were travelling home to Gloucester along the A417. After passing through Stanford in-the-Vale they noticed a very bright light pacing the car. About a mile from the junction with the A361, John, the driver, stopped the car and climbed out.

The light was now overhead and attached to a disc-shaped object, which landed behind some trees. The two women in the car urged John to get back inside, which he did, and they drove away. From then on an air of unreality pervaded the minds of the family. When they arrived home it was much later than it should have been.

Strange frightening dreams followed, and eventually the adults sought hypnosis regression therapy. What emerged was more than a medical examination. It was a story about a dying planet and inhabitants that were fleeing to Earth in the hope of settling here.

The reports of UFO abductions are on the increase across supernatural Britain. But should we take them at face value, or is there something even stranger at work?

The Haunted Home of the Wesleys

Religious Conflict

DURING THE EIGHTEENTH CENTURY Epworth Old Rectory was at the centre of high-powered religious and political fervour. It is just this kind of atmosphere that creates the conditions for poltergeist and other paranormal activity.

The Wesleys took over the parsonage towards the end of the seventeenth century, at a time of official antipathy to both Non-Conformists and Catholics. John Wesley, the founder of Methodism, afterwards produced a faithful record of all that had gone on.

Samuel Wesley was the new rector of Epworth. The family had deep convictions that often conflicted with the establishment views in Church and political matters. In 1662, under the Act of Uniformity, Samuel's grandfather, Bartholomew, was ejected from the church at Charmouth in Dorset. A worse fate befell Samuel's father when he was taken from the vicarage of Whitchurch in Devon and imprisoned for failure to use the Book of Common Prayer.

Susanna Wesley, the new rector's wife, also came from a family fraught with trouble. Her father, Dr Samuel Annesley, vicar of St Giles, Cripplegate, in the city of London, was also ejected in 1662.

Although Susanna had a mind of her own, like her husband she threw in her lot with the established Anglican Church. Yet Susanna's attitude was still independent enough to cause trouble between the couple in 1701, when legislation was enacted to ensure that the Hanoverian line would ultimately occupy the British throne. Susanna refused to say 'Amen' at the end of a prayer for the King, and her husband left her for twelve months before returning to the rectory. The subsequent haunting was seen as divine punishment for Susanna's disrespect for King William. However, the parish were on her side and supported the opposing Stuart cause. Their anger drove them to burn down the parsonage in 1709, but it was rebuilt before the end of the year.

THE HAUNTED HOUSE

John Wesley recorded the first paranormal incident in 1715, when he was about thirteen. On the evening of 2 December, a manservant named Robert Brown was sitting in the dining room with one of the maids when they heard a knock on the door. Robert opened it but there was no one there. This happened several more times, when the sound was accompanied by a groaning.

As Robert went upstairs to bed he was astonished to see a handmill grinding of its own accord. The servant went to bed and was scared out of his wits when he heard the loud gobbling of a turkey, followed by the sound of someone stumbling about in the room. The following day they told the dairymaid about the manifestations, but she did not believe them. That evening, however, she was placing some butter on a tray when a knocking started from the shelf where the milk was kept. As she investigated the knocking became louder, and she fled.

This was the beginning of the manifestations that befell the family and staff over the next two months. The resultant chaos was the complete antithesis of the strict and orderly routine of the household.

The same night that the dairymaid was frightened, Molly, one of the daughters, had an experience whilst reading in the dining room. She heard the door from the hall open, followed by the rustling sound of a dress as an invisible person entered and walked

Epworth Rectory

around her. Molly calmly stood up and left the room. After supper, in their bedroom, Molly light-heartedly told her younger sister, Sukey, what had happened. As she spoke a knocking sounded from under a table, and the iron-framed casement began clattering. The girls discovered that a former resident of the rectory named Jeffery had died there; thus the haunting was believed to be the work of 'Old Jeffrey'.

Later that week Hetty, another sister, heard heavy footsteps coming down the stairs from the attic and going past her. The eldest sister, Emilia, heard a noise 'like a person throwing down a vast coal in the middle of the kitchen' as she locked up for the night. When she investigated, there was nothing amiss. Emilia 'chased' a knocking sound around the hall and kitchen the following night. Finally she was pushed against a wall when a door violently flew open.

Mrs Wesley was sceptical of the claims made by her children and staff, but when Emilia appeared a few days later and begged her to come to the nursery all that changed. There had not been a cradle in the nursery for years. Yet as they stood outside the door they heard the unmistakable sound of a cradle being violently rocked on the wooden floor.

The rector, too, was sceptical and scolded his wife for going along with the beliefs of the children and servants. But that evening, while he was saying prayers before the assembled household, a violent knocking began which travelled around the room. This happened every evening from then on, at precisely the moment when he mentioned the new Hanoverian King George. The haunting seemed to be directly connected with his wife's earlier refusal to recognize William as the King of England.

When another clergyman, Mr Hoole, the vicar of nearby Haxey, came and said prayers to subdue Old Jeffrey the respite was short-lived. The Revd Wesley then threatened the entity with a pistol and it turned its attentions to him, in one instance knocking him against a wall.

The phenomenon developed its power and began to make itself visible. Mrs Wesley saw something 'like a badger but without any head' run under Emilia's petticoats. The creature was also seen by others in the parsonage, including Robert Brown who thought it resembled a rabbit. Animal squeaks were sometimes heard, and a maid was alarmed by a noise like a death rattle. The Revd Wesley grew so terrified that he wrote to his eldest son imploring him to come to Epworth. But as he was preparing to leave for home, John received another letter telling him that the manifestations had stopped.

THE ISLE OF AXHOLME

The landscape around Epworth is flat, with an atmosphere not shared with any other part of Britain. Indeed, with its criss-crossing of dykes the area resembles Holland more than England.

Epworth was originally the centre of the Isle of Axholme. The area from Luddington in the north to Gunthorpe in the south was locked in by marshes and rivers including the Trent, Don and Idille. The destruction of trees on the Isle by the Romans increased flooding, so that nearly 100 square miles were under water during certain times of the year.

All that changed in 1609 when a Dutchman called Cornelius Vermuyden was in the entourage of Prince Henry, eldest son of James I. They were hunting deer in the marshes and the

Dutchman had the idea that they could be drained. An agreement was subsequently drawn up between Charles I and Vermuyden. Dutch engineers were brought over and work commenced, but it was not entirely satisfactory and violence erupted because the islanders were angry at their loss of rights. Even in the Wesleys' day many places could still only be reached by boat.

Hauntings After the Wesleys

Although the supernatural violence of those two months was never repeated, strange events did not end there. Colin Barton, the current warden of the rectory, told me: 'There seem to have been a number of less significant happenings since those years. Emily Wesley became Mrs Harper and moved to London in 1750, where she was conscious of "Old Jeffrey" haunting her there.'

A local historian called Stevenson recorded: 'More than one hundred years after the Wesley family had left the rectory house, the then resident rector heard extraordinary noises there, which induced him to take his family away for a time to the Continent.'

Colin Barton also told me of more recent cases:

One local resident told my wife that the ghost had left the Old Rectory in 1956, when the Methodist Church had the building renovated and restored. Apparently the ghost went to a farmhouse. What has happened to the ghost we do not know, because the farmhouse has since been pulled down and today two modern houses stand on the site.

I have been told, quite reliably, that a few years ago a young man saw an apparition in the garden that looked like an old man in clothes of a bygone age. It disappeared as he walked over to see it, and the youth was very disturbed by the event. Occasionally we hear noises about the house, as if someone were walking around. It is quite common to get odd noises in an old home, so we do not take it very seriously!

THE EPWORTH LEY

LEYS

Leys are invisible lines of power which criss-cross the earth and go through prehistoric mounds. Many of these mounds lie beneath churches and castles built in more recent times. Alfred Watkins, who wrote about leys in the 1920s in his book *The Old Straight Track*, discovered that ancient standing stones, neolithic burial grounds and churches were in exact alignments. To qualify and to rule out chance, a ley must pass through at least four points.

It is interesting to note that many haunted places seem to reside on leys. For instance the Ram Inn, page 95, and Falmouth, page 118. Glastonbury Tor, page 110, lies at an intersection of several leys.

A ley 11 miles long starts – or ends – at Epworth church (SE 781038). It travels through Owston Ferry church (SE 805003), Castle Hill (SE 805002), Jenny Hurn (SE 816986) and Springthorpe church (SK 875897).

Consult Ordnance Survey map 112.

How to Find Epworth and the Old Rectory

Come off the M62 at Junction 35 and take the M18. Then join the M180 at Junction 5. Come off at Junction 2 on to the A161 going south. Epworth is three miles down this road.

If coming from Doncaster, get on to the M18 going north. Come off at Junction 5 and join the M180. Then follow directions as above.

On entering Epworth, turn left at the crossroads and continue past the Market Cross to the T-junction. Turn left into Rectory Street and you will find the Old Rectory on your left. Street parking is easy; there is also a central car park and toilets.

In the centre of Epworth is the Market Cross where John Wesley preached to the villagers. Across from it is the Red Lion Inn, where he lodged in later years after returning from America.

The Rectory is open to the public and visitors are shown around the building, including the attic room where many of the phenomena seemed to emanate. This became known as Jeffrey's Chamber.

The rectory is open 1 March–31 October, Monday to Saturday 10a.m.–12 noon and 2p.m.–4p.m., Sundays 2p.m.–4p.m. *Tel: 0427 872268.*

Consult Ordnance Survey map 111/112.

NEAREST MAIN TOURIST INFORMATION CENTRE
Central Library, Waterdale, Doncaster, South Yorkshire, DN1 1JW. *Tel: 01302 734309.*

OTHER PLACES HAUNTED BY POLTERGEISTS

The village of Binbrook lies to the north of Market Rasen and Louth in Lincolnshire. It can be reached by taking the B1203. During the beginning of 1905 poltergeist activity was operating around Binbrook Farm. The Revd A. C. Custance of Binbrook Rectory prepared a report for the Society for Psychical Research on the case.

Objects were thrown around and were transported from room to room, small fires started around the building. A servant girl sweeping the kitchen continued her task unaware that her back was alight. The owner, Mr White, saw what was happening and smothered the flames with wet sacks. She was then taken to Louth Hospital.

Even more bizarre were the attacks on Mr White's chickens. During January 1905 he lost 226 birds. Something tore the skin away from their necks and snapped their windpipes. The hen-house was watched night and day but whenever it was examined four or five *more* birds were discovered dead.

A most unbelievable poltergeist took over a farm run by the Irving family at Cashen's Gap on the Isle of Man in 1932. The case was investigated by Captain M.H. MacDonald. The phenomenon apparently masqueraded as a talking mongoose! It made scratching noises behind the oak panelling, sang hymns and talked in several different languages. MacDonald recorded many incidents while he was there. According to researcher John Hall, the farm no longer exists.

HIGHWAY TO HELL?

A SINISTER LANDSCAPE

CAN THE DISRUPTION of the natural landscape cause strange things to happen? Could the building of a new road release supernatural phenomena into our world? That is what seemed to happen in September 1987 when construction of the Stocksbridge bypass was underway. Events continue even in the present day.

Stocksbridge is a small town a few miles north of Sheffield, surrounded by rugged moors, reservoirs and woodland. It lies in a deep valley surrounded by steep escarpments rising almost 2,000 feet above sea level. This southernmost corner of Yorkshire is beautiful and sinister, a place where modern high-tech civilization nudges uncomfortably with nature at its rawest, where winter winds and blizzards wreak their havoc undefeated. It is a place where the supernatural seems the most natural thing in the world.

CLOSE ENCOUNTER ON LANGSETT HILL

On 19 September 1987 Len Marsh went to his niece's wedding in Stocksbridge, and afterwards visited his sister there. He left for home in Manchester at 9.25p.m., driving along the A616. As he reached Langsett Hill, just three miles from the town centre, for no

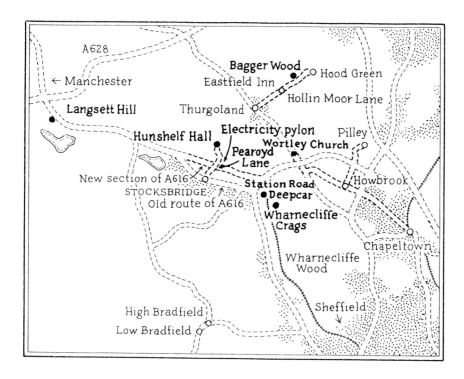

obvious reason he slowed the car right down. It was dark on the road, but unusually, it was totally deserted. A voice inside of him said, 'take your time'.

There was a pine forest on his left, and Len found himself looking at the trees through the passenger window. Suddenly a bright red light in a clearing caught his attention. Then he saw that there were strips of light, alternatively coloured red and white, pulsating, and giving the impression that they were attached to a circular object about 50 feet off the ground.

A hundred yards further he pulled into a lay-by. He thought about going back on foot to get a better view, but he was afraid, and decided instead to carry on with his journey. Curiously, during the whole time he sat there he does not remember seeing another vehicle. When he turned left on to the A628, the traffic was normal.

When he arrived home his wife was pacing the floor. By his reckoning it should have been around 10.10p.m. In fact it was 11.10p.m. What had happened during the missing hour? Had Len really sat in his car the whole time, or had he been somewhere else? After the incident Len started having dreams in which he saw a grey face with large black eyes. He also saw himself, standing in the pine forest, looking up at a brightly lit circular object. Were these suppressed memories, or imagination?

GHOULS ON THE HIGHWAY

Len Marsh did not know it at the time, but just days before, a different drama had unfolded two miles back on the new section of the road.

At that time the A616 went right through Stocksbridge, but it was in the process of being diverted through the rocky crags overlooking the town. One of the ancient moorland roads which was being disrupted by the £14 million bypass was Pearoyd Lane. A bridge was under construction to allow the lane to pass over the new road. At that time the central structure had been built, but it was not linked either side with the lane. Without ladders or scaffolding it was not possible to climb on to the bridge.

Near midnight on 7 September two security men, Steven Brookes and David Goldthorpe, were driving along the closed road. As they neared an electricity pylon they saw four or five small beings, which they took to be children, dancing in a circle between the struts. They stopped their vehicle and climbed out, but the 'children' had vanished. There were no footprints in the fresh mud.

They continued their patrol and, as they neared the uncompleted bridge, saw a hooded figure on the parapet. Goldthorpe put his vehicle's lights on main beam, but the rays passed right through the figure. It too disappeared, and the men were so upset that at 7a.m. they roused a local vicar and begged him to carry out an exorcism. Michael Lee, their boss, saw them and later testified that they were terror-stricken. The matter was reported to Deepcar police station, where it was greeted with scepticism. But all that was to change.

EXORCISM

Exorcism is practised by the Christian Church to drive out spirits and there is an exorcist in every diocese. The Church of England performs about ten exorcisms a year but apparently these often serve only to antagonise the phenomenon, which then increases its activities.

WHAT'S ALL THIS, THEN?

On the Saturday night of 12 September, a week before Len Marsh's experience, PC Dick Ellis and special constable John Beet were on patrol. They decided, without informing anyone, to drive up near Pearoyd Lane. It was a clear, moonlit night. They parked facing the bridge, on which stood a white painted pallet box. After a few minutes they became aware of a 'shadow' flitting across it and around the back. They drove nearer and had a look around. Nothing was amiss. The officers returned to their original position – and lo and behold, the 'shadow' reappeared!

Ellis, who was in the driving seat, had his window wound down. Suddenly a horrible chill coursed through him, and he had a feeling that someone was standing by the side of the car. He turned his head and saw a figure wearing light clothing, with a V on its chest. Then it vanished, and simultaneously reappeared on the passenger's side. Beet screamed out and hit his colleague on the arm. His description differed markedly from PC Ellis's.

To Beet, it was a 'man' wearing Dickensian clothing. The being just stared in at him, and then Beet found it hard to focus and it was gone. When the pair tried to contact Deepcar police station by radio, there were loud thumps on the back of their car.

THE SIGHTINGS CONTINUE

Lorry driver Melbourne Heptinstall had just pulled off the road into Deepcar in 1990 when he had a creepy experience. He stopped in the trailer park in Station Road, and while removing the ropes from the trailer he suddenly went cold. Then he noticed a horrible musty smell and saw a monk-like figure gliding through his headlights.

June Beevers, a psychic from nearby Penistone, became convinced that sightings of the hooded figure were proof that the road had disturbed the spirit of a monk. Her belief was based on her own experiences and a legend. According to the story a monk from Hunshelf Hall died, but his wish to be buried in Stannington was ignored. Instead he was buried in unhallowed ground somewhere near the bypass. His grave had been disturbed during the construction work.

GHOST MONKS

Apparitions of monks seem quite popular as evidenced at Chingle Hall, page 12, Netley Abbey, page 150, Lindisfarne Castle, page 142, Northumberland, and Snowshill Manor, Gloucestershire.

The best documented case was investigated by noted author Colin Wilson and involved a Cluniac monk hanged for rape in the time of Henry VIII. Witnesses of high repute observed the phenomenon in the Pritchard household in Pontefract, Yorkshire during the 1960s.

In another well-known case, architect Frederick Bligh Bond was put in charge of excavating Glastonbury Abbey in 1907. A keen spiritualist, Bond contacted several deceased monks through automatic writing. They provided him with detailed plans of the former Abbey, which subsequent excavations proved correct. (See also page 110.)

The psychic claimed that, while travelling on the road, she felt a presence in the seat next to her. There was a big black shadow in the passenger seat that transmitted fear to her. Eight of her clients had made similar reports to her of the monk-like figure.

On another occasion June was driving along the bypass when she saw the shadowy figure in a car in front of her. When she tried to overtake the vehicle, the ghost disappeared.

In 1992 Elizabeth Howard from Chapeltown was driving along the bypass with her boyfriend. They both suddenly smelt smoke, like strong pipe tobacco. Elizabeth was bemused as neither of them smoked and no one else had been smoking in the car.

ROAD OF DEATH

The new section of the road opened on a Friday the thirteenth in 1988. In only five years there have been many serious accidents and eight deaths. Sheffield and Hillsborough MP Helen Jackson called for the bypass to be officially declared an 'accident blackspot'. The accidents were blamed on design faults, and in 1994 alterations were planned to make the road safer. But June Beevers believes the accidents are caused by the ghost. Only time will tell.

OTHER HAUNTED ROADS NEAR STOCKSBRIDGE

The publicity surrounding the bypass encouraged people who had suffered experiences on other nearby roads to come forward.

Janet Bennett and a companion were travelling on the road between Wortley and Chapeltown in 1967 when she saw a hooded figure. It was a misty Friday night when suddenly the dark outline of a hooded figure appeared before her car, then quickly disappeared into trees.

Graham Brooke was training for the London Marathon in the autumn of 1987 when he and his son Nigel also sighted something on the same road. They were coming back down from Wortley church when they saw a figure in eighteenth century dress with a dark brown cape and carrying a bag with a chain. Their hair stood on end and they were aware of a musty smell reminiscent of an antique shop. Then it just disappeared.

In 1948 Stanley Beaumont of Burncross and a friend saw the ghostly figure of a woman on the road between Pilley and Howbrook.

A taxi driver and his wife experienced an apparition on Hollin Moor Lane between Thurgoland and Hood Green. Mr Cullin of Kendray first saw the ghost when he was driving alone, but on a second occasion he had his wife Diana and their three children with him. It was a Wednesday night in 1993. They had just come over the hill from the Eastfield Inn when Mr Cullin saw a 'shadow' come over a wall and cross the road in front of the vehicle. He slammed on the brakes and they all watched it vanish into Bagger

Wood. Mr Cullin said: 'It floated above the road, and it was like a white shape covered with a piece of cloth which dropped down like a policeman's cape.' When he reported the incident to Wombwell police station, they said they had also received a call from another witness.

ALSO NEARBY – THE DRAGON OF WANTLEY

On the southern tip of the town, Wharncliffe Crags tower over Wharncliffe Wood. The Crags are popular with climbers and walkers, and there are several footpaths leading through the woods and over the top of the rocks. Below the rock face is a cave said to have been a dragon's lair in medieval times. The 'Dragon of Wantley' was slain by 'More of More Hall', who wore a suit covered in sharp spikes. The beast had been terrorizing the area, eating everything in sight: children, cattle and even trees. More hid in the Dragon's Well before launching his attack, which lasted 'two days and a night'. He supposedly dispatched the beast by kicking it in its testicles!

There is a lot of controversy over the source of the legend. The Mores can be traced back before 1100, and their coat of arms,

---

DRAGONS

There is a tradition of dragons around the world, and drawings of dragons, which resemble dinosaurs, were made hundreds of years before the discovery of dinosaur fossils. Dinosaurs could not have existed in the Dark Ages, so were dragons a paranormal manifestation, an echo of creatures which once ruled the Earth? If 'ghosts' can form out of 'ectoplasm', why not other creatures?

Not all dragons possessed scales and wings, some were depicted as giant worms and were often linked to bodies of water. Included amongst these are the Worm of Spindleston Heugh (Northumberland), the Dragon of Aller (Somerset), the Lambton Worm (Durham), the Ludham Dragon (Norfolk), the Mordiford Dragon (Herefordshire) and St Leonards Forest Dragon (Sussex).

dating to Norman times, depicts a green dragon. Three miles west of Wharncliffe Wood, along a network of minor roads, is the village of Bradfield. The twelfth-century church of St Nicholas is sited directly below an ancient Celtic burial mound, and is a prime example of a Christian church built on top of a pagan temple. Seen from above, the earthwork is crudely serpentine in shape. On the north-east corner of the church is a dragon carved in stone, five feet long, with flapping wings and yawning mouth.

Bradfield is also where 'Robin of Locksley' (Loxley) – Robin Hood – was born. There are several wells named after Robin Hood and Little John in the Sheffield area.

How to find Stocksbridge

Come off the M1 at Junction 35a, on to the A616. Probably the best place for an overnight vigil is on the bridge spanning the bypass which links Pearoyd Lane. This is accessed from the town.

Follow the road out of Stocksbridge on to Langsett Hill. Len Marsh had his experience in or near the wood on your left, a quarter of a mile before the junction with the A628. There is a pub at the crossroads.

See map on page 57 and also consult Ordnance Survey map 110.

NEAREST MAIN TOURIST INFORMATION CENTRE
Peace Gardens, Sheffield, South Yorkshire, S1 2HH.
Tel: 0114 2734671/2734672.

OTHER HAUNTED ROADS NATIONWIDE

Blue Bell Hill in Kent is notorious as a location where motorists have encountered apparitions. Over the years there have been more than a dozen recorded incidents. The sightings have been linked with two fatal accidents. The first, in 1965, involved a bride-to-be and three attendants; in the second, in 1967, two girls were killed in a car crash.

In 1974 bricklayer Maurice Goodenough was convinced he had run over a ten-year-old girl. He wrapped the bloody body in a blanket and called the police. In the interim period the child vanished. Around the same time Richard Studholme, lead guitarist of the seventies group Chicory Tip, picked up a girl and dropped her off at West Kingsdown. She asked him to deliver a message to her parents at nearby Swanley. When he called there, Richard discovered the girl had died on Blue Bell Hill some years before.

Blue Bell Hill lies on the A229 between Chatham and Maidstone, and beside the road are two Neolithic monuments. The road also runs over a prehistoric graveyard.

Another 'haunted' road runs between Frome and Nunney in Somerset over Gibbet Hill. In 1977 a decorator picked up a middle-aged man in a check jacket who sat on the back seat of his car, and vanished en route. Other drivers reported feeling a 'presence' in their vehicles, and many reported sightings of an apparition on the road to Frome Police. Police confirmed that witnesses were often in shock. These sightings seem to go back to at least the 1940s. Nunney is just ten miles west of Warminster (see page 102).

East Anglia

CLOSE CALL IN THE WOODS

THE SECRET OF RENDLESHAM FOREST

*D*ID A UFO LAND close to two RAF NATO bases in December 1980? Certainly there are official records of mysterious lights and an object seen near the bases by military personnel. But off-the-record comments led ufologists to investigate the possibility that a close encounter had occurred between a crashed or landed object and American servicemen.

RAF Bentwaters and RAF Woodbridge lie in the heart of Rendlesham Forest. At the time of the alleged incident they were NATO installations leased to the USA. Now, with the demise of the cold war threat, the bases are shut down.

Rendlesham Forest itself is a large managed woodland area along a stretch of the East Anglian coastline known as the Sandlings. Prior to acquisition by the Forestry Commission, most of the area was heathland with just a few belts of conifers and hardwood trees. Planting began during the 1920s and 1930s. Felling and replanting took place in 1975, when Corsican pine replaced the original Scots pine. This was the situation when on Boxing Day something apparently crashed through the canopy of trees and alerted men in the nearby bases.

FROM OUT OF THE BLUE

The case has been investigated and written about extensively by ufologist Jenny Randles in her books *Sky Crash* and *From Out of the Blue*. She and other investigators painstakingly pieced together this remarkable story.

Sometime after midnight on Friday, 26 December, Gordon Levett was standing outside his cottage in the hamlet of Sudbourne attending to his dog when he noticed an intensely bright light overhead. It resembled a giant mushroom, sitting on an oval plate. It was white, tinged with green, and completely soundless.

As he watched, Gordon became aware that the dog was shaking with fright. Seconds, minutes, later the strong light drifted away in the direction of RAF Bentwaters. The dog never did recover, and within weeks was dead.

Forty miles north of Sudbourne, at 1a.m. a radar station near Norwich tracked an object the size of a Boeing 737 heading on a south-westerly course from out in the adjacent area of sea known as the Wash. The operators checked, and discovered that no one knew what the object was. Indeed, it was also being tracked at two other bases as it headed down the coast past Lowestoft. Suddenly the blip disappeared, as if it had gone down – right over Rendlesham Forest.

One hour later two security guards positioned at the end of the Bentwaters' runway spotted a light hovering in the trees. At first they thought it was illumination from Orford Ness lighthouse, but the lighthouse was a few degrees further south. One of the men called the base, where it was decided to send out some back-up.

Two men went into the forest to investigate, and saw red and blue lights through the trees. They wondered if they were dealing with a downed aircraft. Suddenly they were in a clearing – not a natural one – but one newly created as if something had smashed through the tree canopy. The expected aircraft was not there, but something else was.

According to the American airmen, the object was about the size of a car, similar in shape to an Apollo space capsule, and stood on tubular legs. It was lit up like a Christmas tree with blue, white and red lights. When one of the men walked towards the thing, it rose a few feet into the air and drew away. They followed the object as it expertly dodged between the trees into a field beyond. Suddenly it sped away, pouring out light which sent a herd of cows into a panic. The men were found by a search party at 3.45a.m. wandering in the forest in a daze. As the incident had happened on British soil the duty commander called in the police, who took a statement. Later, impressions in the ground were found which corresponded to the position of the object's legs.

At 10.30 that night lights were once more spotted through the trees. Four men, one of them armed, were despatched to investigate. They approached the phenomenon, which was so brightly illuminated with yellow, red and blue lights that no shape could be discerned. There was a fog or mist rolling underneath it. When the men drew closer, the thing backed away as on the previous occasion. The men withdrew and contacted Lieutenant Colonel Halt at the base, who instructed them to remain at the edge of the forest and wait for him and a party of reinforcements to join them.

A FULL-SCALE SEARCH

Just after midnight a convoy of trucks containing thirty men arrived, and a thorough search was made. But something seemed to be interfering with several of the vehicles' engines, and the powerful searchlights which the team were trying to set up in the clearing. They were cutting out as if something was draining power from them. The lighted object, however, seemed to have gone.

An investigation was set up, which involved taking radiation readings and measurements of the holes made by the tripod legs. The search and investigation were tape-recorded, and later an edited version was released to ufologists. At one point high radiation readings were recorded. The investigators talked about a 'blast' area, and abrasions on nearby trees. Samples were taken away for analysis.

While the crash/landing site was being examined, another team of men were searching the forest for the source of the lights. They were in a clearing near the house of a gamekeeper called Vic Boast when suddenly a yellow/green mist started to form. The mist began to pulsate and then a red light appeared through the trees, heading towards the phenomenon. Cows in a nearby field began to bellow, and a few hundred yards away Halt and his team heard the cacophony. Halt's reactions are clearly recorded on the tape.

A call came through from the other men, and now Halt's team too could see the red light. They had no doubt that they were dealing with a UFO. As they edged closer, the animals stopped bellowing. One of Halt's men declared that the object was about four feet off the ground, and very large. It was also heading their way, and 'pieces of it' were 'shooting off'.

In the meantime, the team who had first spotted the phenomenon stood in terror as the red light entered the clearing and silently exploded with brilliant luminescence as it made contact with the mist. As the light diminished, a machine or craft of some sort was seen to be standing on the ground; it glowed, and was triangular with a domed top. The men took some photographs and made to surround it, but as on the previous occasion it lifted up and moved away.

Halt and his men watched and became aware of two other strange lights. Suddenly the objects flew off in the direction of Orford Ness. Then suddenly the observers saw a strange object coming over the trees towards them. Halt's reactions were recorded on the tape. Beams of light were emitted from the thing, which hit the ground. Then it too took off into the night.

WHAT REALLY HAPPENED IN RENDLESHAM FOREST?

That story was pieced together from statements by servicemen speaking off the record, and by civilians living nearby who also observed the strange lights. Other information was gleaned from the tape recording and a memo written by Halt two weeks later. The latter was released not by the Ministry of Defence, but by the US government under their *Freedom of Information Act*. It clearly records the sighting of strange lights and the close encounter on 27 December between servicemen and a 'triangular metallic object' 'three metres across and approximately two metres high'.

Of course the entire scenario could have been a fabrication to

---

THE UFO COVER-UP

There is a continuing cover-up of information about UFO incidents by the authorities. This was proved when the USA passed their *Freedom of Information Act* in 1979. Released documents showed that, despite denials, the FBI and the CIA had retained an active interest in the phenomenon. The cover-up is probably because government will not admit it cannot understand nor control the phenomenon, although some researchers believe officials are in secret communication with UFO entities!

---

cover up the crash of a secret experimental aircraft belonging to either NATO or the former USSR. Sceptics came up with the silly explanation that all the witnesses had been fooled by the light from the Orford Ness lighthouse. But even if some of the servicemen were new to the base and likely to misidentify the light, local people would not have confused it with lights zipping around the sky.

Whatever the truth, the area where the ground traces were found was shortly afterwards cleared of trees. Were the trees due for clearance anyway, or was it connected with the events of December 1980? Was the evidence of a UFO crash being removed?

How to Find Rendlesham Forest

Rendlesham Forest is near the village of Woodbridge just a few miles north of Ipswich. Take the A12 from Ipswich and follow the signposts.

After the devastation caused by a hurricane during the night of 16/17 October 1987, broad-leaved species including oak, chestnut and birch were added to Rendlesham Forest. In recent years the area has been opened up to the public with the construction of nature and cycle trails, car parking, picnic areas and toilet facilities. There is also a camping and caravan site in Rendlesham. Visit Rendlesham Forest where possibly one of the most momentous events in human history occurred!

Consult Ordnance Survey map 156.

NEAREST MAIN TOURIST INFORMATION CENTRE
Town Hall, Princes Street, Ipswich, Suffolk, IP1 1BZ.
Tel: 01473 258070.

OTHER AIRBASES INVOLVED IN UFO INCIDENTS

Several airbases around Britain have been involved in UFO incidents. Indeed, Bentwaters and RAF Lakenheath were the targets
for UFOs in August 1956. Multiple radar and visual contacts were
made of round, white, rapidly-moving objects that changed direction abruptly.

American Air Force personnel at Bentwaters made the initial
sightings on radar. The information was passed to Lakenheath,
fifteen miles north west of Bury St Edmonds. Lakenheath reported
a bright light travelling at 'terrific speed' over the base, at about the
time a C-47 over Bentwaters was buzzed.

An RAF Venom night fighter was scrambled from RAF
Waterbeach near Cambridge. The aircraft chased a bright light for
thirteen miles before losing it. He was then vectored on to a new
target ten miles east of Lakenheath. As they closed in the object
suddenly and swiftly arced over the fighter to a position behind it.
Cat and mouse manoeuvres followed. When a second Venom was
scrambled, the UFO disappeared as if it had grown tired of the
game.

This case even made some sceptics rethink their position. Radar
expert Gordon Thayer concluded in an official report: 'This is the
most puzzling and unusual case in the radar-visual files. The
apparently rational, intelligent behaviour of the UFO suggests a
mechanical device of unknown origin as the most probable explanation'.

UFOs seemed to take an interest in Operation Mainbrace, a
NATO exercise which took place over several days during
September 1952. One of the objects appeared over RAF Topcliffe,
near Thirsk in North Yorkshire. At mid-morning on 19 September
a round silvery object hovered over the airfield. Many ground
crew and civilians watched the object which was rotating and
wobbling slightly. A Meteor jet was scrambled and the pilot con-

firmed the description. The object gathered speed and disappeared from view.

I interviewed Flight Lieutenant Cyril George Townsend-Withers about his close encounter on a clear and sunny winter's day in 1953. He was testing a new experimental Canberra aircraft which took off from an RAF test base on Boscombe Down in Sussex. They went up to 55,000 feet, which was a record, and were cruising over Salisbury Plain just after noon when their radar picked up an object five miles behind them.

Townsend-Withers saw the bright silver craft. The Canberra tried to out run it, but it maintained its distance so the pilot then did a U-turn which put them on a collision course. The object was enormous and metallic, a kind of thin disc with small tailfins. Suddenly it climbed vertically at a fantastic speed without leaving a vapour trail. Townsend-Withers and his crew knew that no terrestrial aircraft could have carried out that manoeuvre...

THE HAUNTING OF BORLEY

THE MOST HAUNTED PLACE IN BRITAIN?

IN THE ANNALS of the supernatural no place has more of a reputation for being haunted than the village of Borley in the northernmost tip of Essex. The alleged manifestations originally centred around Borley Rectory and were brought to the attentions of the public by controversial psychic investigator Harry Price.

Borley today is a scattered village of around a hundred inhabitants. Its name is derived from the Anglo-Saxon *barlea*, meaning 'boar's pasture'. Its earliest records date back to 1042, when a freeman named Lewin owned Borley Manor during Edward the Confessor's reign. In 1066 William the Conqueror gave the manor to his half sister Adeliza, the Countess of Aumale. It is also mentioned in the Domesday Book of 1086.

GHOSTLY NUNS AND OTHER PHENOMENA

The Revd Henry Bull built the notorious rectory (pictured on page 74) on the site of a much older building in 1863. Before that a Benedictine abbey is said to have stood there, although proof is lacking. In 1900 Henry's four daughters were in the rectory grounds where they saw a phantom nun. She was seen by others

Borley Rectory

on subsequent occasions, and the location became known as the Nun's Walk. Many years later Price was to unearth the bones of a woman in the cellar of the building. During a seance it was claimed that, three hundred years earlier, a nun was murdered by a member of the wealthy Waldegrave family.

When Henry Bull's son Harry died in 1927, many witnesses claimed to have seen his ghost walking the rectory corridors. During the next six months about a dozen clergymen and wives viewed the house with the intentions of taking up residency. All of them declined. However, this probably had more to do with the damp and miserable condition of the ugly redbrick building than with any supposed ghost.

The Revd Eric Smith and his wife lived there for nine months in 1928–9 and it was during this time that Price made his appearance. The Smiths were prepared for local superstition and rats, but not for unexplained footsteps, showers of coins, strange knockings and other odd occurrences. Mrs Smith is also supposed to have seen a phantom coach and horses on the drive. Although the Smiths remained sceptical, many of the phenomena happened in the presence of other witnesses, including Harry Price.

Things really hotted up when the Revd Foyster and his young wife Marrianne moved into the rectory in 1929. Heavy poltergeist activity started, which included messages addressed to Mrs Foyster scratched on the walls. When Guy L'Estrange, a Justice of the Peace, visited the house in 1932 he afterwards wrote an account of crockery smashing and bottles flying through the air. He was convinced that trickery was not involved. Price thought otherwise. He had come away from Borley a year earlier convinced that Marrianne Foyster was responsible for many of the 'phenomena'. Subsequent investigation into her background seemed to reinforce that conclusion. Ironically, Price, who earned his reputation for exposing fake mediums, was himself to be condemned as a trickster.

OTHER FAMOUS PARANORMAL INVESTIGATORS

- Sir Oliver Lodge, Sir William Crookes and Sir William Barrett – Victorian scientists who investigated the 'afterlife'
- Professor Hans Bender – a German psychologist and director of the state-run parapsychology laboratory at the University of Freiburg
- Dr Raymond Moody – a pioneer in near-death experience research
- Maurice Grosse and Andrew Green – specialists in the poltergeist field

---

WAS PRICE RESPONSIBLE FOR SOME OF THE HAUNTING?

Later investigations by Price were condemned by those who accompanied him as peppered with fraud. Harry Price had a love of being in the public eye and openly courted the media. He wrote two best-selling books on Borley Rectory, and it was in his interest to keep the story rolling. After his death, three members of the Society for Psychical Research – Dingwell, Goldney and Hall – carried out a thorough investigation. They concluded in a book published in 1956 that Price, along with others, had created much of the myth.

It may be true that Harry Price and others hyped up the phenomena, but there are enough independent records of sightings of apparitions and other anomalies to conclude that Borley Rectory was indeed haunted. In February 1939 the rectory was mysteriously burned down, a fate which had been prophesied eleven months earlier during a seance. However, some concluded it was the work of the then current owner who wanted to collect the insurance money.

The noted investigator Andrew Green visited Borley in 1951 with members of the Ealing Psychical Research Society. In his book *Our Haunted Kingdom* Green describes how one member grabbed his arm in terror, and pointed to a woman in a long white gown whom he could see at the end of the Nun's Walk. No one else could see the apparition, although Green heard rustling in the undergrowth as if someone were walking through it.

Ley expert Stephen Jenkins claimed that Borley church stands at a node where four lines cross. Jenkins was photographed by his wife on 1 December 1979 against the south wall of Borley churchyard. When an enlargement was made, several people independently noted faces in nearby trees.

Two years earlier on 28 August, Jenkins and his wife Thelma were on the minor road north of Belchamp Walter Hall, just two miles from Borley. At precisely 12.52p.m. they were driving along when four men appeared instantaneously in front of the car. They were hooded and cloaked in black, and carrying an old-fashioned coffin. The couple noted the absolute physical *reality* of the tableau. The men disappeared into a gap in the hedge, but not before the couple had caught sight of the face of one of the figures – it was a skull.

The following day they returned and took a photograph at exactly the same time. When the film was processed, Jenkins was astounded to find a short-cloaked figure with a skull-like dome in the scene. There was nothing at the location to account for the image.

BORLEY CHURCH

The controversy that surrounded Borley Rectory has not tarnished Borley parish church, reputedly also haunted. While everyone was concentrating on the rectory, the church was neglected. Ethel Bull told Price in 1929 of an incident in the nineteenth century when coffins in the Waldegrave vault beneath the church were discovered to have been moved. Ghost hunter Peter Underwood believes that, with the destruction of the rectory, the phenomenon transferred itself lock stock and barrel to the church; but it was probably there all along.

A wooden church constructed at the time of the Norman Conquest pre-dated the current building. Twelfth-century flint and rubble has been discovered in the south wall of the nave. In the fifteenth and sixteenth centuries rebuilding took place and parts were added to the main structure. In the churchyard lie the graves of the Bull family.

Psychical investigators began to take an interest in Borley again during the 1960s. At this time a small group of researchers from Harlow conducted a series of late-night vigils over several years. During that time they heard a series of bangs and knocks and the sound of heavy furniture being moved around the church. When they attempted to record the noises, the group found their tape recorder smashed and the tape torn from its reel.

While in the orchard across the way they were confronted by something huge and dark 'like an animal' which banged loudly on the fence. At 3a.m. on another occasion they heard 'laughter and merriment which seemed to be coming up the road towards Borley church'. Yet there was no one on the road, and a search of the area by car drew a blank. Further confirmation of the corporeality of the nun was obtained by Geoffrey Croom-Hollingsworth and Roy Potter. They were in the orchard facing the Nun's Walk when, according to Croom-Hollingsworth, 'Suddenly I saw her quite clearly, in a grey habit and cowl as she moved across the garden and through a hedge.'

The investigator wondered if it was a hoax – the figure had disappeared into a garage. He called out to Potter, who was on the road. As Potter joined him, they both saw the 'nun' reappear through the far wall of the garage. 'She approached to about twelve feet from us,' said Croom-Hollingsworth, 'and we both saw her face, that of an elderly woman in her sixties, perhaps. We followed her as she seemed to glide over a dry ditch as if it wasn't there, before she disappeared into a pile of building bricks.'

In 1974 film director Denny Densham obtained permission to

SPECTRAL LADIES

Many places are noted for their spectral Grey, White, Black and Pink Ladies.

Grey Ladies have been seen in Abbey House, Cambridge and Shute Barton House, Devonshire. A Lady in Black is said to haunt Windsor Castle; at Coughton Court in Warwickshire a Pink Lady has been seen; and in the medieval house of Cotehele, Cornwall, lurks a Lady dressed in White.

carry out a series of vigils in the church with sophisticated recording equipment. The machines picked up unidentified noises and the unmistakable sound of a heavy door being opened and slammed shut, with the squeaking of a rusty bolt.

On a subsequent visit the equipment was set up as normal and a search of the building made. Half the team were locked inside and the rest remained on guard in the churchyard. 'Suddenly,' Densham said, 'there was a curious change in the atmosphere. One of the team felt as if he was being watched, and we all felt very cold.'

Recorded on the tapes were the usual knockings and rappings, and the crash of the door again; then, unexpectedly, a human sigh. This was subsequently broadcast in a BBC documentary, and is quite chilling. A tape in a small cassette machine was discovered unravelled.

Heavy footsteps were picked up on other occasions, even though the stone floor is carpeted. On their final visit the team saw a glow of light by the chancel door and heard a horrible grunt. Members of the Enfield Parapsychical Group also heard strange noises and a deep grunting voice.

There has been no major investigation of Borley in recent years. However, in 1986 two people visiting the village heard footsteps passing on the road, even though no one was visible.

Researcher Steven Ironmonger told me of a lady who regularly cleaned the church. One day she was carrying out her duties as normal when she heard an unusual noise from behind. Turning around, she was astonished to see the wooden candelabra suspended above her, twisting and turning on its chains. It was as if it was caught in a fierce wind – but there was not even a draught.

There is something strange about the village of Borley, but neither the current rector nor the other residents will talk about it. They prefer to play it down, not wishing to encourage sensation seekers. The site of the former rectory now contains three bungalows and an orchard, but the church is still there to visit. Over the years, regrettably, there has been some vandalism, so please treat Borley and its villagers with respect. Otherwise, spend a pleasant afternoon there soaking up the atmosphere and taking photographs. Who knows what might turn up on them?

How to Find Borley

From Bury St Edmunds, take the A134 for 18 miles to Sudbury. A few miles before the town centre, take a right-hand turning that leads to Melford Hall. Continue south for two miles, then turn right and look for signs to Borley and Foxearth.

If coming from Ipswich, take the A1071 to Sudbury and then follow the A134 north for six miles. Look out for signs on your left.

Consult Ordnance Survey map 155.

NEAREST MAIN TOURIST INFORMATION CENTRE
6 Angel Hill, Suffolk, Bury St Edmunds, IP33 1UZ.
Tel: 01284 764667/757083.

OTHER HAUNTED CHURCHES

The fifteenth-century church of St Decuman has a supernatural tale associated with it. It is situated on a small hill overlooking the Somerset coastal village of Watchet. Nearby is Kentsford Manor, which was once the home of the distinguished Wyndham family.

When Florence Wyndham died, the sexton decided to steal her rings. He waited until dark then set off for the family vault in the church. But others had the same idea, and he was waylaid by a gang of ruffians who forced him to let them into the church. They made him remove the rings before making their escape. Then, suddenly, Florence Wyndham sat up in her coffin.

According to the story, the sexton told the rector what had occurred, then died of shock. Florence is said to haunt Kentsford Manor.

St Peter's Church near Preston Park in Brighton was the location for a ghostly encounter in the 1970s. A couple walking in the churchyard met a lady dressed in medieval costume. Thinking she was in fancy dress, they spoke to her but received no reply. Realising there was no sound of footsteps from the woman, they turned around to see her fade into nothing.

A few miles north west of Ashford in Kent lies the village of Pluckley. The church there has been the scene of several ghostly happenings. A white dog has been seen in the building, and in 1975 witnesses observed a woman in a long white gown gliding among the tombstones.

Central England

THE GHOSTS OF CROFT CASTLE

IMPORTED APPARITIONS?

THE SITE OF CROFT CASTLE, on the Welsh border, was the property of the Croft family from the time of the Domesday Book until 1957, except for the years 1750–1923. Nowadays the castle is owned by the National Trust, although the family still live there.

Its ancient walls and four round castellated turrets of pink stone date from the fourteenth and fifteenth centuries. Modifications were made during the sixteenth and seventeenth centuries, while new ceilings and a Georgian Gothic-style staircase were added in the mid-eighteenth century. Some of the interior panelling has come from other old houses. If ghosts are psychic imprints on wood and stone, could this account for the plethora of apparitions at Croft Castle? Are some of the ghosts *imported*?

OWEN GLENDOWER

Researcher Peter Underwood recorded many close encounters during interviews with past and present occupants. Does the ghost of Owen Glendower haunt Croft Castle? There have been a number of sightings of an enormous 'man' clothed in leather, taken to be the Welsh folk hero.

A friend of Sir James Croft had a sighting in the 1920s. He was playing billiards, in what is now called the Oak Room, when he

---

FAMOUS GHOSTS

People often claim to have recognised ghosts as famous historical figures. Here is a selection:

- Charles I, Anne Boleyn and Henry VIII have been sighted at
  Windsor Castle.
- In the grounds of the Petit Trianon, Versailles, two English
  women saw Marie Antoinette in August 1901.
- Rudyard Kipling's ghost has been seen in the house and
  garden of his former home 'Bateman's' in Burwash, East
  Sussex.
- Sir Winston Churchill has appeared at Chartwell, Kent,
  which was his home for forty years.

See also *The Tower of London*, page 131, for other famous ghosts.

---

turned and saw a ghostly figure of a huge man in leather. A cousin
also encountered an unfamiliar figure in the room during that
time. She thought it must be a workman because of his rough
clothing, but as she watched he faded.

Around 1926 some of the Oxford University boat crew were
staying at the castle for the weekend. When one of their number
came downstairs for dinner he saw in the Portrait Gallery a man
over seven feet tall, with bobbed hair and wearing a leather jerkin.
As he watched, the figure faded until nothing remained.

Later, some of the guests were preparing to leave for a hunt ball
with their hosts, Sir James Croft and his family. Everyone was
outside climbing into cars when one of the guests remembered he
had left his cigarettes in the Oak Room. He ran back inside, and as
he entered the room almost collided with an enormous man who
almost instantly vanished. His friends afterwards attested that the
big, strapping oarsman was 'green and shaky all evening'.

SPIRITS ON THE LOOSE

During the 1920s the young men and women of the house would
often play card guessing games with their friends in what is now
called the Saloon. Sometimes the games involved the occult, with

activities including table turning and experiments with a planchette – a board standing on rollers through which a pencil is mounted, making contact with a sheet of paper. The operator rests his or her hand lightly on the board and relaxes, allowing an entity to control the muscles and produce messages or answers to questions.

Apparently things got out of hand when the experiment seemed to release a psychic force into the building. On one evening the players were startled to hear a tapping sound simultaneously on the windows of the Saloon, the Oak Room, Blue Room and the Library. Even the dogs were distressed. At the time Sir James was toying with the idea of pulling down the Elizabethan wing. One of the messages read: 'Croft must not destroy Croft.'

AN UNINVITED GUEST

There would seem to be an apparition in Elizabethan costume haunting Croft Castle and the surrounding countryside. In 1949 the *Leominster News* produced a report of a figure in Elizabethan dress seen on Bircher Common, two miles from the castle.

During a fancy dress party in the 1920s one of the guests spotted someone whom they thought was a gatecrasher. She told several of her friends, who all observed the figure mingling with the guests. None of them recognized the man, who was very elaborately dressed in Elizabethan costume. When someone decided to question the interloper, he had disappeared. Afterwards, those who had seen the figure said he bore a strong resemblance to a portrait of a previous Sir James Croft who had died in 1591.

GHOST STORIES

In the late 1950s when the Croft family were trying to collect enough money for the endowment without which the National Trust could not take over the property, they received a large sum from a Welsh lady interested in the eighteenth-century Croft family. She had come to England for her sister's funeral and on the way home decided to call at the castle. After parking her car she walked around the exterior. It was a warm, still summer's evening. As she drew near the Saloon, she heard some beautiful eighteenth-century music being played from within. At that time the castle was empty. Ironically, the room is now used for concerts.

Croft Castle has many visitors, including parties of schoolchildren. One day in October 1978 the assistant custodian was talking to a head teacher in the hall. Suddenly the teacher spun round. He said that while they were talking he had seen, in the reflection of a glass case, someone walking across the room. The assistant custodian, who was facing in that direction, saw nothing.

The most recent case on record involves a twelve-year-old grandson of the family. He told his grandmother that he had seen 'a little old lady in black' going into a bedroom. The grandmother investigated, thinking it might be an illusion created by shadows, but found no evidence of this.

What is it about ancient buildings that produces so many ghosts? Do buildings really act like batteries, storing images created by the emotional energy of their occupants? Or is there something in these places that can pick the minds of people and produce images of what is in them?

ALSO NEARBY – WEOBLEY CHURCH

Weobley is approximately eight miles south-west of Leominster, off the A4112. There is a tradition that the Devil can be conjured up by anyone walking slowly around the preaching cross in the churchyard and reciting the Lord's Prayer backwards.

How to Find Croft Castle

Croft Castle is just six miles north of Leominster. From Leominster take the B4361, then turn left on to the B4362. The castle is two miles further on your right. If travelling on the A49, going north or south, look out for the B4362 turning on the west side of the road. Croft Castle is also signposted from the A4110.

This is a beautiful part of the country. Apart from the castle, the estate also boasts a spectacular Iron Age hill fort, in use between the fourth century BC and AD 50. On a clear day there are views over fourteen counties.

The surrounding parkland is available to visitors all year, but the castle is open May to September, Wednesday to Sunday and Bank Holidays, 2–6p.m. April and October, Saturday and Sunday 2–5p.m. Easter Saturday, Sunday and Monday, 2–6p.m., but Closed Good Friday. *Tel: 0568 780246.*

Consult Ordnance Survey maps 148 and 149.

NEAREST MAIN TOURIST INFORMATION CENTRE
Castle Street, Ludlow, Shropshire, SY8 1AS. *Tel: 01584 875053.*

OTHER HAUNTED CASTLES OVER THE WELSH BORDER

There are several castles in Wales which are supposedly haunted. Carew Castle near Pembroke boasts the apparition of a woman in white seen wandering through the ruins. Visitors also claim to have seen a young girl wearing a blue-grey apron scurrying from the Great Hall in Penhow Castle near Newport.

A goggle-eyed woman with a disproportionately large head allegedly haunts the ramparts of Caerphilly Castle. She is known as the Green Lady because of her green robes and veil. Sometimes she is accompanied by soldiers in chainmail. Tourists and staff have described an apparition which bears a resemblance to the second Marquess of Bute who died in the chapel. A figure wearing a red cloak has been seen in the hall, on the stairs and by the chapel doorway.

'White Ladies' are associated with Oystermouth Castle near Swansea Bay and Ogmore Castle on the bank of the Ewenny River near Bridgend in Mid Glamorgan. This latter spectre guarded some treasure hidden beneath the floor of the tower. One story tells how she allowed a man to find a pot of golden guineas. Appearing before him, she told the man he could keep half of the money provided he left the rest buried. He agreed, but returned later for the remainder of the pot. The White Lady caught him in the act and attacked him with nails sharpened like claws. He went home telling people he had been injured in a drunken brawl, but confessed the truth when a mysterious illness overtook him. He is said to have slowly wasted away.

According to records a man in a gold-laced hat and suit appeared to a spinning woman in Powys Castle. The spectre, which opened and closed doors like a normal person, led her to a box hidden beneath the floorboards and instructed her to send it to the Earl of Powys in London. She did this, and the Earl rewarded her with free accommodation for the rest of her life. No one knows what was in the locked box. The incident was recorded in 1780 by Wesleyan Methodist preacher John Hampson, who investigated the case and interviewed the old woman.

THE WITCH MURDER OF LOWER QUINTON

THE SINISTER CHARLES WALTON

DURING RESEARCH for a previous book I came across the bizarre murder of a man called Charles Walton. It occurred in the village of Lower Quinton, just a few miles south of Stratford-upon-Avon, in 1945. The village sits in the shadow of Meon Hill. The area is steeped in witchcraft, and surrounded by place names such as Devil's Elbow and Upper and Lower Slaughter.

Walton, a hedger and ditcher, had something of a sinister reputation in the village. He lived in a thatched cottage with his niece. Loners in small rural communities attract suspicion and gossip as a matter of course, but Walton, unwittingly perhaps, courted the darker emotions of his neighbours.

Outwardly he was just a labourer who did work for several local farmers. Donald McCormick heard things about Walton during research for his book *Murder by Witchcraft*. Apparently this grizzle-haired, droopy-moustached man bred huge toads. One villager told him that Walton took to harnessing the toads to a miniature plough which he placed on seeded fields. Three hundred years earlier, a self-confessed witch by the name of Isabel Gowdie described how she used this same method to magically stunt the

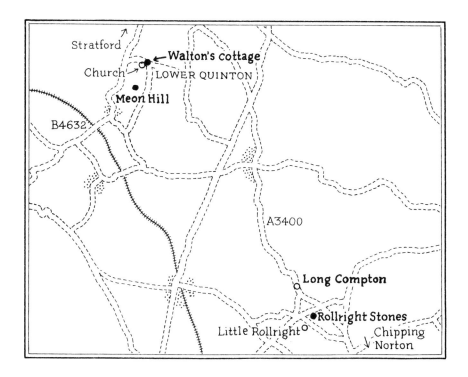

growth of crops. Had the old man fallen out with one of his employers, and was he using witchcraft to get his revenge?

It was said that Walton could accurately imitate the call of birds – and understood every 'word' they said. He described how birds would perch on his hands and shoulders, flying off to any place he indicated. Despite this empathy with animals, the sight of a black dog (see page 20) sent a chill of fear through him. This supposedly stemmed from a frightening boyhood vision.

For three consecutive nights the young Charles Walton had seen a phantom dog running across Meon Hill. On the third night he stared in terror as it transformed into a headless woman. The following morning his sister died. This experience changed him from an outgoing, talkative youth into a brooding introvert. Unfortunately for the elderly Charles Walton, or because of him, the year of 1944 was a bad one for the villagers of Lower Quinton.

Things started to go wrong, and the finger of suspicion was pointed at Walton. Despite an early spring, crops has been slow in growing and there were several mishaps with livestock. Beer went sour in the local pubs, and the harvest was every bit as bad as had been expected. The stage was set to mirror an earlier drama played out in a neighbouring village.

The Long Compton Witch Murder

In 1875, a seventy-five-year-old woman from Long Compton was murdered by a man called John Heywood. The community had suffered a series of misfortunes, and Ann Tenant had become a focus for blame. Heywood, referred to as a village idiot, believed there was a coven operating in the area. Given the chance, Heywood admitted, he would have 'killed them all'. His confession shows he had no doubts that Ann Tenant was practising black witchcraft: 'Her was a proper witch. I pinned Ann Tenant to the ground before slashing her throat with a bill-hook in the form of a cross'. The poor woman had been staked to the ground by a pitchfork.

A Ritual Sacrifice

On 14 February 1945, Walton was discovered on his back under a willow tree on Meon Hill. A pitchfork had been driven through his neck with such force that it had pierced the ground to a depth of six inches. A cross had been carved from the neck to the lower abdomen, and the bill-hook which had been used to carry out the job was still wedged between his ribs. The parallel between the two killings is plain to see. This was not just a murder. It had been carried out by someone with an intimate knowledge of the occult and had the hallmarks of a ritual sacrifice.

It was believed that a witch's power lay in his or her blood. Suspected witches were 'blooded' – cut to release their 'supernatural' powers. Unfortunately, the release of blood often meant the release of life too, as in the case of Walton and Ann Tenant.

The day of Walton's death, 14 February, is not only St Valentine's Day and occasionally Ash Wednesday, but also the date when the ancient Druids carried out sacrifices to ensure good crops. Author Colin Wilson speculated that the old man's murder was probably planned months in advance, to undo the damage he had supposedly done through the practice of evil ritual. Could Walton have been sacrificed by a group or an individual with pagan beliefs? Certainly it was someone who was familiar with the earlier murder.

THE POLICE INVESTIGATION

No one was ever convicted of the killing. A team led by Detective Superintendent Robert Fabian of Scotland Yard took some four thousand statements and sent twenty-nine samples of blood, hair and skin to police laboratories for analysis, but to no avail. The locals were less than helpful. A few days after the murder, a black dog was found hanged on Meon Hill. Did someone believe the animal was Charles Walton's familiar? Fabian himself saw a farm hand chasing a black dog which ran out of sight, but the boy denied there had been a dog. A police car ran over a dog, and other animals began to die during the investigation.

'FAMILIARS'

The concept of the witch's 'familiar' came during the seventeenth century. It was believed that a witch's pet, usually a cat, crow or toad, was an imp in disguise – a henchman who could shape-shift and carry out the witch's bidding. This 'familiar' was supposed to have been presented to the witch by Satan himself.

See also *Pendle*, page 18.

It was, to say the least, a rum affair. Walton was not the victim of a casual killer, but possibly the focus of a successful attempt to purge the village of a practising witch. At least that was what anthropologist Dr Margaret Murray thought. If so, the clandestine witchfinders of Lower Quinton knew exactly how to cleanse the area. All this happened in 1945 – but it might just as well have been 1645.

TRACKING DOWN THE PAST

The story so intrigued me that I knew I had to visit Lower Quinton. Before I entered the village, my vision was captured by the brooding slopes of Meon Hill – the sacrificial altar for the life of Charles Walton. Its patchwork skirt and wooded dome swathed in mist were an arresting sight.

Lower and Upper Quinton are full of beautiful Cotswold cottages, with a duckpond and parish church, and a modern housing estate on the periphery. The streets are crowded and narrow and full of atmosphere. My enquiries in the College Arms and the Gay Pig met with undisguised hostility. The murder could have happened yesterday. It was like being on the set of a *Hammer* horror film. I decided to call on the vicar to see if he would show me Walton's grave, and perhaps furnish me with details of the crime. But when I stepped outside there was a wedding in progress.

The matter was firmly closed. Half a century had passed and people were as uncooperative now as when the police investigation was under way and McCormick was asking questions. The only person who would talk to me was a man drinking in the British Legion Social Club. He told me that there had been a feud between Walton and another man called Potter. It was Potter who found the body. The witchcraft connection came about partly because an ancestor of Walton's had been burned as a witch in a nearby village during the Middle Ages.

For years afterwards, Detective Inspector Fabian used to hide up on Meon Hill on the anniversary of the killing. He was working on the theory that a murderer always returns to the scene of the crime. No one ever did turn up, and if it was Potter, he went to the grave with the secret.

Was Charles Walton's death a ritual killing connected with local witchcraft? Certainly the case made a lasting impression on Fabian. In 1976, now in retirement, he commented to Charles Sandell of the *News of the World*: 'Detectives deal in facts, but I must admit there was something uncanny about that investigation.'

ALSO NEARBY – LONG COMPTON AND THE ROLLRIGHT STONES

Long Compton – where Ann Tenant was killed – is 15 miles south of Lower Quinton on the A3400, just four miles north of Chipping Norton. There is an old saying in the village: 'There are enough witches in Long Compton to draw a wagonload of hay up Long Compton Hill.' Today there are stone and thatched cottages, antique shops and the remains of a medieval cross.

Just south of the village, near Little Rollright, are a circle of Neolithic or Bronze Age stones known as the Rollright Stones (see photograph 5 opposite page 24). A larger stone nearby is said to have been a king, and the circle, his courtiers. They were said to have been turned into stone by a witch, who was then changed into an elder tree. On Midsummer Eve people would gather at the tree and cut into it. As the sap oozed the King would move his head. Modern witches still gather in the circle and conduct rituals.

In 1978 the stones became the focus of the Dragon Project. This was a scientific attempt to measure and identify energies said to be emitted by the Rollright Stones and similar phenomena, and it met with some success. Dowsers have claimed for some time that energy lines emanating from the stones criss-cross the landscape.

How to Find Lower Quinton

Take the B4632 south from Stratford-upon-Avon and after about five miles look for signposts on your left.

See map on page 89 and also consult Ordnance Survey map 151.

NEAREST MAIN TOURIST INFORMATION CENTRE
Bridgefoot, Stratford-upon-Avon, Warwickshire, CV37 6GW.
Tel: 01789 293127.

OTHER BLACK MAGIC SITES

There are certain places and buildings in Britain which have strong connections with black magic.

West Wycombe Park and Church are bisected by the A40 running from High Wycombe. Sir Francis Dashwood, owner of the park, founded the Knights of St Francis in around 1755. They became known as the Hellfire Club, notorious for occult rituals and mass orgies attended by some of the top dignitaries in the country. Dashwood rebuilt the church, which was situated inside an earthwork. Here the Hellfire Club sometimes met. They also used a system of underground caves for their activities. The baronet built a mausoleum where he was interred in 1781.

The ruins of St Mary's Church at Clophill in Bedfordshire are also of interest. In the 1960s and 1970s the ancient graves were desecrated and the bones used in rituals. When researchers Janet and Colin Bord visited the site, they claimed they felt 'an over-whelming evil atmosphere emanating from the church and graveyard'.

Occultists can be blamed for causing powerful atmospheres. The philosopher, scientist and occultist Dr John Dee moved to Kempnough Hall, in Worsley, Manchester for seven years in 1589 and may have left his mark. A subsequent tenant called Sam Derbyshire went berserk for no apparent reason and hacked his wife to death and murdered his son. Other tenants experienced an atmosphere and witnessed apparitions.

Dee, together with his partner, an occultist called Edward Kelly, allegedly brought a corpse to life in St Leonard's Churchyard at Walton-le-Dale in Lancashire in 1560.

See also Boleskine House on the shore of Loch Ness, the home of Aleister Crowley, page 168.

THE ANCIENT
RAM INN

SAVED FROM THE BULLDOZERS

THE GLOUCESTERSHIRE country town of Wotton-under-Edge has in its midst a historical, archaeological and supernatural gem. The first Ram Inn was built in 1289, but was destroyed by fire along with much of the village. The current building probably dates from the fourteenth or fifteenth centuries, with some parts added in the nineteenth. Over the years little has been done to change its half-timbered structure. On the contrary, when John Humphries bought the building in 1968 it was in a dilapidated state. Not long after John moved in, however, he learned that the local council had put a compulsory purchase order on the property. They wanted to knock it down to widen the road! John started a hard campaign, and it was his determination plus the will of the local people which forced the council to back down.

This relic of the past still possesses an essential primitiveness. BBC programme-makers must have realized this quality when they chose to use the inn for location shots during filming of the historical drama series *Poldark* in the late 1970s. In recent years a number of television crews have filmed there, as its reputation has grown for being 'haunted'.

A COLOURFUL PAST

The Ram Inn, John discovered, had an exciting history. He himself uncovered a priest's hole and a bricked up tunnel which allegedly once led to St Mary's parish church opposite. Two of England's last highwaymen hid out in the inn, and the building was notorious for several murders. Perhaps this explains the Ram's spooky reputation.

A local dowser told John there were bodies buried beneath the foundations. With the help of an archaeologist he dug up the floor of one of the rooms and recovered the bones of several children, along with two broken ceremonial daggers. At about that time John also discovered an ancient Saxon map which clearly showed that both the inn and the church were within a circle created by buildings and the surrounding streets. This perfect circle is still evident on a modern map.

The circle is an archetypal symbol that has featured heavily in folklore and religion from pagan times. It is a unified and complete figure without beginning or end. As a magical symbol, from fairy rings to modern crop circles, it has always been with us. Occultists attempt to conjure up demons within a magic circle while they protect themselves inside a triangle.

There is a further link in the chain. Leading down to the church, and in line with the inn, are a series of steps carved into the hillside. At one time these terraces were used by monks for the cultivation of vines, although they are much older than that.

Steps leading to a high place on which sacrificial altars were erected were a feature of pagan times, especially in Egypt, the source of many modern witchcraft beliefs and rituals. Height is also connected with spiritual superiority: the soul of a departed king or shaman (priest) would rise up the staircase to a higher plane. John Humphries believes that the area within the circle in Wotton-under-Edge was an ancient pagan sacrificial site.

The idea of a ram features in the Bible's best-known story of sacrifice. In Genesis 22, Abraham is tested when God orders him to sacrifice his son. He relents at the last moment, and instead Abraham kills a ram caught in a thicket.

According to John, a ley passes through the high place, the

The Ram Inn

church and the Ram, supposedly adding to its power. With its bloody history, and these other connections, it is not surprising that the Ancient Ram appears to be the playground of unusual phenomena.

ASSAP INVESTIGATES

I visited the Ram Inn as part of an investigative team from the Association for the Scientific Study of Anomalous Phenomena. We carried out an all-night vigil, with members stationed in the various rooms of the old building. We had with us specialist cameras and sensitive recording equipment and, although nothing outrageous occurred that night, some interesting things were experienced and noted.

A photograph taken in the living room by Lyn Tungate had smoky images on it even though nothing odd was seen at the time. Whilst in the Bishop's Room – allegedly the most haunted place in the building – Mel Turford and I both independently recorded a

sudden drop in temperature. This phenomenon was repeated
when Lyn Tungate and Barbara Russell were in the room. The
room was miked up, and at this point a loud crackle was recorded
on the tape. Later that night, as Mel went to enter the now empty
room, he had the distinct impression that 'someone' opened the
door for him from the other side. More recently, a digital thermometer recorded a temperature drop from 18 degrees Centigrade
to 6.8, then finally to minus 6.8!

During a follow-up vigil, while John was attempting to raise the
ghost in the Beaufort Room, several investigators felt a distinct
coldness close to him. The following morning, a female investigator alone in the room heard a male voice say: 'Wakey, wakey, it's
time to get up!' On another occasion, while a local youth was
sitting on a chest he felt something grip the back of his neck; he
shot up, cannoning into an investigator. That old chest has a reputation for strange occurrences.

John Humphries was the victim of many odd experiences, both
alone and with witnesses. Dozens of guests have signed declara-
tions that things have happened to them. John blames many of
the phenomena on the portrait of John Wesley, the founder of
Methodism, which hangs near the staircase. The Wesleys had their
own poltergeist at Epworth Old Rectory in South Yorkshire (see
page 48).

PERSONAL EXPERIENCES

This is the statement of a woman who stayed several nights in the
inn with her partner in November 1984.

At around 12.20a.m. in the Bishop's Room, whilst Steve was
out, I was aware that something strange was about to happen. I
was drawn towards the fireplace where I saw a wispy white mist
which developed into the outline of a man. I was so frightened
I pulled the covers over my head. I did not look again until Steve
returned, by which time the apparition had disappeared.

Nothing else happened until later in the night. Then I felt a
presence all around me. I tried to move my arms and open my
eyes, but I couldn't. Someone or something was trying to pull

me out of bed. I started to shout, which awoke Steve who then grabbed me, and the presence disappeared.

In the early hours of the following evening I awoke several times with my pulse racing for no apparent reason, except I had an impression that the sheets were being pulled towards the foot of the bed.

Included in the plethora of phenomena observed over the years are:

1. Apparitions including a monk, a cavalier and a young girl.
2. A very real sensation of 'something' climbing into bed with experients.
3. Footsteps which followed two men after they ran out into the street.
4. Whispering, disembodied voices.
5. Individuals thrown about the main sitting room.
6. Sudden temperature drops.
7. Items mysteriously moved from one location to another.
8. Various items of electrical equipment operating 'by themselves'.
9. Objects observed floating about rooms.
10. A strange mist (ectoplasm?) forming inside the building.
11. Strange balls of light moving about the rooms.

ALSO NEARBY

Newark Park is just a mile east of Wotton, reached on a minor road leading to the hamlet of Ozleworth. The historic building and its extensive grounds were given to the National Trust in 1949. Its reputation for being haunted has been investigated on several occasions with some success.

Peter Underwood and members of the Ghost Club recorded on tape the sounds of disembodied voices, rustling and footsteps. Other investigators have experienced sudden drops in temperature, windows being violently rattled, tapping noises and the inexplicable movement of objects.

How to find the Ancient Ram Inn

Wotton-under-Edge is approximately 18 miles south of Gloucester. Come off the M5 at Junction 14 and follow the B4509, then turn left on to the B4058 in Wotton. All traffic into the town must come to the war memorial crossroads. Take the downhill road to Potter's Pond. The Ram is at the bottom on the right-hand side, and the entrance is at the rear of a large car park. Although the Ram is now a private residence, John Humphries will conduct interested people around the building for a modest fee.

Consult Ordnance Survey maps 162 and 172.

NEAREST MAIN TOURIST INFORMATION CENTRE
Subscription Rooms, George Street, Stroud, Gloucestershire, GL5 1AE. *Tel: 01453 765768.*

OTHER HAUNTED INNS

Old inns seem to be a draw for the supernatural. Perhaps it's the hustle and bustle of such places that creates the necessary energy?

Poltergeist activity broke out in 1985 at The Bull's Head on Chorley Road, Swinton, near Manchester. Staff and customers variously experienced apparitions, the levitation of a stool, footsteps, strange voices on the telephone and the operation of light switches. The climax came during the early hours of Easter Monday when two men were apparently attacked in the ancient cellar. One was taken to hospital concussed and had eight stitches to a head wound.

Supernatural events began to plague the fifteeth-century Black Horse Inn in Cirencester, Gloucestershire, during 1933. On 13 August Ruby Bower, the niece of the landlord, woke up in the night aware that something was wrong. The room had been recently altered, yet she saw windows which no longer existed. Worse, she saw an apparition of an old woman gliding across the floor wearing old-fashioned clothes. The name 'James' was discovered behind the new panelling, scratched on to the glass of the old window. A psychic claimed she detected the trapped spirits of an old man and woman. On her instructions the pair were exorcised.

South-West England

THE WARMINSTER 'THING'

FOCUS OF BIZARRE EVENTS

THE SMALL COUNTRY TOWN of Warminster first hit the head-lines in 1965, and for the next few years it generated stories which appeared in newspapers across Britain and the United States. The place drew thousands of tourists from many countries who wanted to experience, first hand, the Warminster 'Thing'.

Warminster sits on the edge of Salisbury Plain, where army manoeuvres are practised, just 15 miles to the west of Stonehenge. Twenty miles south of Bath, it is surrounded by the rolling Wiltshire hills. The town is dominated by one particular tor – Cley Hill – where sightseers gathered to watch for strange phenomena.

What was special about Warminster, that it should become the centre for UFO sightings, close encounter experiences and weird poltergeist activity? Or was much of it down to hype and fraud?

THE 'THING' ARRIVES

At 1.25 a.m. on Christmas Day 1964 Mildred Head, the wife of a former police officer, was woken by a noise 'as if twigs were brush-ing the tiles, or like a cat sharpening its claws'. It developed into a noise which she described 'as giant hailstones pelting down with all their might'. Mrs Head looked outside to find the weather clear,

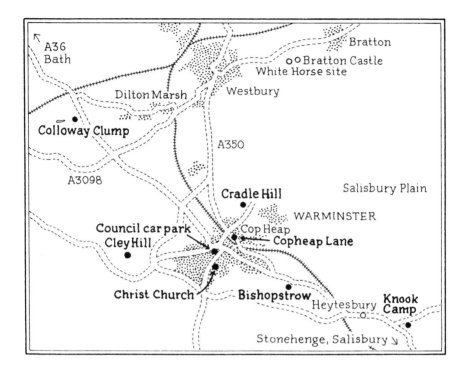

'yet a storm was raging on the roof'. She also noticed a humming sound which then faded.

Postman Roger Rump was awoken by a terrific pounding on the roof of his house. As he stirred into consciousness it sounded as if the tiles were being rattled and torn off. Later, when he checked, nothing was amiss.

At 6.12 a.m. that day Mrs Marjorie Bye was walking to Christ Church in the town to take part in Holy Communion. Suddenly in the still morning she heard a frightening crackling noise in the air above her. A terrible droning caused her to quicken her step, but before she had time to reach the church wall it was upon her. A terrible pressure bore down on her head, neck and shoulders, causing paralysis. When the effects wore off she stumbled, weak and stunned, into the church.

Around the same time in Knook Camp at nearby Heytesbury over thirty troops of the 1st Welch Regiment were rudely awakened by a thunderous crescendo. A sergeant told one journalist: 'It was as if a huge chimney stack from the main block was ripped from the rooftop, then scattered in solid chunks of masonry across the whole camp.' The guard was put on alert, but there was no evidence of anything outside and nothing developed. The noise was not caused by any conventional aircraft.

Inexplicable bangings, rattlings and explosions haunted many houses over the coming months and years, causing residents to conclude that they were dealing with poltergeist phenomena.

Multiple Sightings

Over the years there have been hundreds of sightings around Warminster. Here are a few of them.

On 28 March 1965, nineteen-year-old Eric Payne was walking home after leaving his girlfriend at Sutton Veny. It had been snowing, but now a heavy fog covered the road. As he neared Bishopstrow on the outskirts of Warminster, close to a school, he became aware of a buzzing noise.

Suddenly the treetops at either side of the road flattened and there was a terrific noise like a can of nuts and bolts being violently rattled. Then he felt pressure bearing down on him. Through all this he was able to make out an oval shape in the mist. The pressure forced him on to the grass verge until it eventually subsided.

Delivery truck driver Terry Pell was taking a load of fruit and vegetables to a depot in Copheap Lane when he had a terrifying experience. At 4.36 a.m. on 10 August 1965, as he neared a bend, a crimson ball of light flew from the nearby hillside to the road, hovered, then put inself on a head-on collision course with his truck.

Pell described it as like a human eye, but bigger than the truck. As he braked he had the impression that the engine had already cut out. The Thing pressed right up to the windscreen as the truck left the road and came to a stop near the signpost to Upton Scudamore. Incredibly his wife and daughter, who were also in the cab, slept through the encounter and only awoke after the UFO had disappeared.

Ten days later Robert Payne and his girlfriend, Wendy Gulliford, were leaving Warminster on the road to Dilton Marsh after a night out. As they passed by Colloway Clump, a group of tall firs near a large reservoir, the engine of Payne's scooter suddenly died.

Two large spheres of silvery light were hovering over the trees and the couple could feel waves of heat hitting them. Then the objects moved away, pirouetted around one another, and returned, even closer. Suddenly they seemed to wink out, and the scooter started without any trouble. Payne said afterwards: 'They were the spitting image of human eyes lit up.' Apart from the effect on the scooter, the terrified couple noted that both their wristwatches had stopped at 11.02 p.m.

Charles Hudd, an employee of Warminster Urban Council, reported for work with four colleagues at the council car park at 4.45 a.m. on 1 April 1966. They were confronted by the sight of a huge, silent, silvery cigar in the sky, travelling from west to east. Just before it reached Cop Heap – the reputed grave of a Saxon chieftain – the thing stretched lengthways and crimson light flooded along it. Suddenly it split and burst apart, emitting a bright flash. The men expected to hear an explosion, but none came. From the rent fell six small red 'blobs'. Suddenly they stopped, changed colour to silver, and sped off northwards.

THE WARMINSTER MYSTERY-MONGER

Chief scribe of the strange goings on was a local journalist named Arthur Shuttlewood. He worked for the *Warminster Journal*, and was instrumental in bringing the stories to the attention of the national and international media. It was he, too, who referred to the phenomenon as the 'Thing'. Shuttlewood wrote several books as a consequence, including the best-selling *The Warminster Mystery*.

He and others came in for criticism and were accused of hyping up the sightings. Several photographs were produced, most of doubtful authenticity. One photograph, taken in March 1970, was part of a hoax designed to fool ufologists – which indeed it did. In 1994 someone claimed that a photograph of a flying top, taken by seventeen-year-old Gordon Faulkner in 1965, was faked. Faulkner denied it. It is obvious that the people of Warminster were the victims of an unusual phenomenon that plagued their town for several years. Details such as the pressure felt by many witnesses, and effects on vehicle electrical systems, dovetail with other UFO events worldwide.

Arthur Shuttlewood entered the corn circle controversy when he announced that he and about fifty other witnesses had observed a circle forming in 1980. He said they were looking across Salisbury Road when the circle formed like a lady's fan opening. The phenomenon was accompanied by a high-pitched humming sound.

LEYS AND ORTHOTENIES

According to some researchers, Warminster has an incredible twelve leys passing through it! French ufologist and scientist Aimé Michel plotted the sightings of UFOs during the 1954 'flap', when a large number of sightings were made over a short time. He found that they too seemed to operate on straight lines, which he called 'orthotenies'. Some orthotenies seemed to overlap with leys. Did this explain the hot spot of activity in Warminster during the late sixties and early seventies? Was it a centre of power? A crack in the universe creating a gateway for things from another dimension – what ufologists call a 'window area'? Or misperception and imagination?

CLEY HILL

This strangely shaped tor has a very colourful history. Beacons were lit on it in the sixteenth century to warn of the arrival of the Spanish Armada. There are indications that in earlier times it was the location for pagan festivals. Modern pagans believe it is a centre for psychic power. Until the early twentieth century it was customary on Palm Sunday to fire the bushes and coarse grass on the hill in order to drive out foxes, hares – and the Devil!

Certain dates are particularly relevant to the supernatural reputation of Cley Hill. On the Ides of March and June, 31 October (Halloween) and 1 November (Samhain, an ancient fire festival celebrating the beginning of winter) strange things have been reported. People out on the hill late at night have seen strange figures silhouetted against the sky, and heard muffled, primitive voices and the sound of singing coming in waves.

CORN CIRCLES

During the 1980s hundreds of circles and more complex configurations appeared in cornfields mainly in the south of England. They were blamed on everything from UFOs and nature spirits to mating hedgehogs!

In September 1991 two practical jokers, Doug Bower and Dave Chorley, claimed they had been hoaxing circles for the past 13 years. They were inspired by the discovery of 'saucer nests' in Australia during the 1960s. However, the simple circle dates back to the Middle Ages and serious researchers believe that the remaining circles represent a genuine mystery. Some suggest that electrically charged vortices might be to blame.

In August 1980 two corn circles were discovered in the lee of the hill. One was nearly 50 feet wide and the other nearly 60 feet. Since that time circles have appeared almost every summer near Cley and Cradle Hill.

When earth light researcher Paul Devereux took an interest in the area he discovered two fault lines passing near Warminster, one right by Cley Hill. He conjectures that much of the aerial phenomena – in particular an orange ball of light which earned the nickname the 'amber gambler' – could be electromagnetic energy released from deep underground.

ALSO NEARBY – WESTBURY AND STONEHENGE

Eight miles north of Warminster, on the A350, is Westbury. Between the town and the village of Bratton on the B3098 lies the White Horse of Westbury.

The horse is carved into the chalk of the hillside to the west of Bratton Castle, an Iron Age hill fort. Indeed the horse itself seems to date from the Iron Age, although it was recarved in 1778. The horse is 166 feet long and realistic-looking. It was once believed that the image could detach itself from the hill and roam around the countryside. If so, was it responsible for the corn circles that appeared in nearby fields in 1980?

The Westbury circles were instrumental in starting off the craze which escalated in the late 1980s. Most of the configurations which have appeared across the country have been explained as hoaxes, but not all. A man called Ray Barnes claimed to have witnessed a circle forming on 3 July 1982. He was standing in a field at Westbury when he observed an 'agency' travelling across the field. Although invisible, it behaved like a solid object. Before disappearing, in four seconds it described a circle some 75 feet across.

About 15 miles to the east of Warminster lies Stonehenge, one of the most famous stone monuments in the world. Argument still rages over who erected Stonehenge – and why. Archaeologists believe that building started around 1800 BC at the end of the Neolithic period, and was finished by the close of the Early Bronze Age, about 1400 BC.

Legend, however, attributes the construction to a race of superhuman giants who brought the stones from Africa and erected the circle in Ireland. In the fifth century AD the wizard Merlin is supposed to have moved the stones to Salisbury Plain. More recently Stonehenge has been linked with the Druids, who used the configuration to generate occult powers. Certainly the blue stones were not from local quarries, but have been traced to the Prescelly Mountains in Dyfed.

The original purpose of Stonehenge is still shrouded in mystery, although there seems to be a connection with sun worship. Author Gerald Hawkins came up with the idea that the stones were a kind of primitive computer for predicting celestial phenomena such as eclipses.

The Druids' Ceremony takes place annually on 21 June. A vigil is kept during the night, and the service begins when the first rays of the rising sun shine on the altar stone. A second service is held at midday.

How to Find Warminster

If travelling from Bath, take the A36 for 20 miles. Travelling from Southampton on the M3, come off at Junction 8 and follow the A303 for 33 miles. Then take the A36 into Warminster. There is free car parking in the town.

See map on page 103 and also consult Ordnance Survey map 183.

NEAREST MAIN TOURIST INFORMATION CENTRE
Central Car Park, Warminster, Wiltshire, BA12 9BT.
Tel: 01985 218548.

OTHER UFO WINDOW AREAS

There are other places around Britain other than Warminster, Bonnybridge (page 180) and Broad Haven (page 205) which have seen concentrations of UFO sightings. One of them is the Pennine region of England which stretches from Cumbria to Derbyshire. The most active parts of the Pennine chain are the moors around Oldham in Lancashire.

'Window areas' are places which seem to attract large numbers of sightings. In the 1970s witnesses in the Pennines described a phenomenon which became known as the 'phantom helicopter'. This was a lighted object which had all the manoeuvrability of a helicopter but none of the noise. The media and police theorised that a helicopter was smuggling in drugs, illegal immigrants or arms for terrorists. The mystery was never solved. Here are just three examples of what was seen.

A young couple on Hartshead Pike on 10 May 1973 at 9.15 p.m. were suprised by something. They had parked near a tower which overlooks Oldham. The silent object was dome-shaped and emitted red, green and white lights as it rotated before flying off.

In the late afternoon of 5 January 1975 a large group of children were playing by a bridge at Uppermill, just east of Oldham. A disc of yellow light with a red light on top suddenly appeared. It swooped quite low and made a humming sound.

Five days later at Lees a glider pilot and his girlfriend saw a light surrounded by other diffused lights moving below the line of hills. It disappeared behind a golf course.

MAGICAL GLASTONBURY

A MAGICAL PLACE

I *VISITED GLASTONBURY* many years ago without realizing its true significance. Even so, there was a sense of its magic as I walked the streets, marvelled at the ruined Abbey and climbed up the tor to the abandoned church (see photograph 6 opposite page 25). The view on a fine summer's morning, across misty vales towards the Mendip Hills, was breathtaking. Glastonbury is central to the Arthurian legend, steeped in fairy lore and the location for modern UFO sightings.

JESUS IN GLASTONBURY

The site of Glastonbury Abbey, according to some authorities such as Lewis and Dobson, was home to Jesus Christ during the years before his ministry. Long before the arrival, the Druids worshipped a god named Esus/Yesu. Was this coincidence, or had they been warned of Christ's coming? Jesus was said to have visited Britain as a boy with Joseph of Arimathea. He built a shelter on the future site of the Abbey and may have visited Cornwall, where the Jesus Well at St Minver commemorates him. In 1867 a woman claimed that its waters had cured her of erysipelas, an inflamation of the skin and tissue which orthodox medicine had failed to arrest.

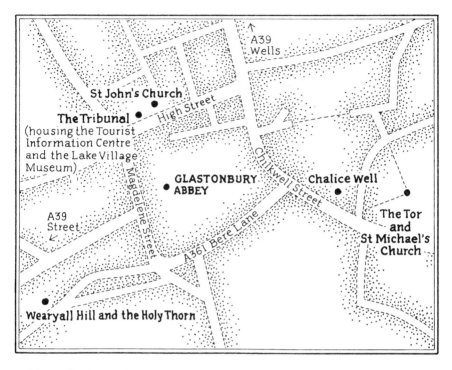

Although the Abbey says nothing of Jesus, it does make much of Joseph of Arimathea. It was he who obtained Christ's body from Pontius Pilate and placed it in a tomb. According to legend, Joseph came to Britain from Gaul in AD 63 on a mission with the apostle Philip. Their boat travelled up the Bristol Channel and along inland waterways to Glastonbury. On Wearyall Hill, Joseph drove his staff into the ground. It grew into the Holy Thorn, which blossomed at Christmas until 1643 when a Puritan cut it down. In 1951 a replacement 'Holy Thorn' was planted, although a descendant of the original still flourishes in front of St John's church in the High Street. It is a variety of hawthorn found in Syria and Palestine, and its white flowers still make an appearance in December and into early spring.

The English king Arviragus gave Joseph and Philip the land where Christ supposedly had made his home many years before. There, in Glastonbury, the Angel Gabriel instructed them to build the first Christian church in Britain. The 'Old Church' was still standing in the early Middle Ages. If the story is true, Joseph must have been very old.

THE ISLE OF AVALON

According to tradition, Joseph is reputed to have brought with him the chalice used at the Last Supper – the Holy Grail, said to have supernatural powers. Centuries later the search for the mythical Grail became interwoven with the story of King Arthur and the Knights of the Round Table.

Glastonbury was surrounded by lagoons and waterways before extensive draining by monks during the Middle Ages. Rising out of the waters was the Tor, towering 500 feet above sea level. Was this the Isle of Avalon – the final resting place of King Arthur? A study of local folk tales, characters' names and the Arthurian legend produced many similarities.

It was in 1190 that the monks announced the discovery of Arthur's grave while rebuilding the Abbey after a fire six years earlier. What they uncovered was a stone slab adorned with a lead cross, on which was written: 'Here lies buried the renowned King Arthur in the Isle of Avalon.' The coffin beneath it was made from a hollowed out log and contained the bones of a tall man, and those of a woman – taken to be Arthur's wife Guinevere.

Is there any truth in the story, or was it just a medieval publicity stunt? The Arthurian legend is set in a brutal period of history which was romanticized, and perhaps this was part of that romanticism. When the area was re-excavated by C. A. Ralegh Radford in 1962–3 he confirmed that the monks had dug where they claimed, and he also found the stone lining of an important grave. Radford's subsequent research went even further towards proving the genuineness of the story. But the relics were placed in a casket by the monks and dispersed when the Abbey was dissolved in the sixteenth century. Today, there is a plaque in the Abbey grounds showing where the bones were found.

THE FAIRY DWELLERS
OF THE TOR

There is a long tradition in the British Isles of fairy folk who dwell in an underworld referred to by some as Annwfn. Portals allow them access into our world, and such a portal is said to exist on Glastonbury Tor.

One story relates to an early Welsh saint, Collen, who lived in a hermitage on the slope of the Tor. He overheard two men talking about Gwyn, king of the fairies, whom they said lived in the hill. Collen scolded them for speaking in such respectful terms of the fairies, as in truth they were demonic. The men replied that Gwyn would learn how offensive his language was.

Not long afterwards a fairy messenger arrived and invited the hermit to go and meet the king. Collen declined, but the messenger returned and issued threats. So he decided to follow the fairy, taking with him some holy water as a precaution.

At the brow of the hill, Collen was amazed to find a castle where no castle had stood before. The king was seated on a golden throne surrounded by retainers, musicians and beautiful fairy women. He offered Collen food, but the hermit declined, suspecting it was drugged. Gwyn then said: 'Have you ever seen men better dressed than these, in their red and blue liveries?'

Collen replied: 'Their dress is good of its kind, but the red is the red of fire and the blue is the blue of cold.' Before Gwyn had time to react the hermit scattered his holy water over the court, and the castle and the fairies all vanished. Collen found himself standing alone on the Tor. St Michael's church was probably built on the hill in an attempt to suppress its pagan reputation.

A further mystery concerns a series of seven terraces that encircle the Tor. The configuration has been compared to prehistoric mazes, which also have seven circuits. Professor Philip Rahtz,

PREHISTORIC MAZES

The symbol of the maze or labyrinth is one of the oldest known to man. It is thought to have originated in Egypt, from where it was brought to Europe by the Crusaders.

Mazes occur in two forms: a spiral with one uninterrupted path, and the Greek meander cluttered with false turns and dead ends. They have always had magical significance, linking this world with the afterlife and death with resurrection.

who excavated the summit during the 1960s, concluded that, if indeed it was a maze, its origins probably lay in the Neolithic era.

The 'maze' is complete except where erosion has destroyed it. It can be traversed by starting from a large stone at the foot of the main path, climbing to the next stone and then turning left, following the terrace clockwise. The final terrace does not quite reach the top, and it has been suggested that it originally led into a tunnel. This concurs with local tradition that the hill is hollow and leads to the fairy underworld.

At the foot of the Tor lies Chalice Well, or Blood Spring (see photograph 7 opposite page 25). Both names connect with the holy chalice, which held wine symbolic of Christ's blood. The well supposedly has healing powers.

MODERN PHENOMENA

That the Tor is 'magical' there can be no denying. Many ufologists see a correlation between fairy stories and contemporary cases of alien abductions. In recent years it has been the focus for strange phenomena.

In 1969 four night shift workers witnessed a saucer-shaped object hovering over the hill. That same year other witnesses saw a fiery red ball. In 1970 a police officer reported the sighting of eight maroon egg-shaped objects in formation above the Tor. Eleven years later, on Midsummer's Day, people climbing the Tor saw a 'dragon-shaped' orange glowing light writhe out of the ruined church tower. It then apparently earthed itself near Chalice Well at the foot of the hill.

Earth light anomalies researcher Paul Devereux believes that such phenomena can be explained in terms of energy fields released into the atmosphere through seismic stress. Indeed, the church was destroyed by an earthquake during the Middle Ages. Devereux had his own sighting whilst on the summit of Glastonbury Tor: he and many other people observed three orange lights.

It was late January 1991 when Ciara Mulford and two friends visited Glastonbury for the day. During the afternoon they decided to climb the Tor. Being young and fit this had never presented a problem on previous trips, but this time Ciara and one of the other girls felt heavy and drained of energy. Descending the Tor they were both startled by a bright flash of orange/pink light which lit up the tower. Strangely, the third girl saw nothing. As they came near to their car, parked at the foot of the Tor, the central locking system suddenly went into operation, locking and unlocking several times.

THE TEMPLE OF THE STARS

More contentious, but just as fascinating, is the claim that the outlines of astrological figures can be traced from the air over Somerset. The Glastonbury Zodiac covers an area 10 miles across. By tracing the lines of the landscape, researcher Katharine Maltwood discovered what she called the Temple of the Stars. The figures vary from one to five miles across, and are roughly analogous to the constellations in the sky. Ms Maltwood, who was led to the discovery through reading an anonymous medieval romance called *Perlesvaus or The High History of the Holy Grail*, published her findings in 1935. The author claims to have used a document from Glastonbury Abbey as a basis for the story.

Critics have commented that the figures are not apparent to the observer unless they have been told beforehand what to look for. They say that supporters will use any feature – including some fairly contemporary ones – to 'manufacture' the outlines. They compare it to the Rorschach ink-blot test, where the subject perceives faces and animal shapes from a random pattern created on a piece of folded paper splashed with ink. However, once they are pointed out on a map, most people agree that the images are quite impressive.

Historical writer Geoffrey Ashe remarks that there is only one previous source which mentions Maltwood's Temple of the Stars. In his prophecies (VI, 22), Nostradamus says:

> *In the land of the great heavenly temple*
> *A nephew at London is murdered through a false peace*

Ashe argues that only the Glastonbury Zodiac could equate with 'the great heavenly temple'. The rebel Duke of Monmouth could have been the 'nephew' who was executed in 1685 by his uncle, James II. The 'peace' was false because James's cohort, Judge Jeffreys, helped overthrow the King three years later. Somerset was the staging post for Monmouth's rebellion, and he encamped his army at Glastonbury.

Whatever the truths of the tapestry of stories woven around Glastonbury, one thing is certain. It was the earliest pagan and Christian centre of Britain – an antithesis of beliefs, one absorbed by the other.

How to Find Glastonbury

If travelling south from Bristol take the A37, then the A39 through Wells, and continue to Glastonbury. Alternatively come off the M5 at Junction 23 and follow the A39 east. From Dorchester travel north up the A37 through Yeovil on to the B3151 to Street, then take the A39 for two miles.

See map on page 111 and also consult Ordnance Survey maps 182 and 183.

Annual Festivals and Events in and around Glastonbury

It was the mecca for sixties' hippies, and today the New Agers have adopted the area as a spiritual centre. During the year a wealth of workshops and events is organized, dealing with shamanism, spiritual healing, herbalism, dowsing, channelling, astrology and numerology. Conducted tours are arranged. Details can be obtained from the Tourist Information Centre listed below. Events are located in Glastonbury, and also in nearby Street and Wells.

The Glastonbury Lake Village Museum, situated in the High Street, is worth a visit, as are the Abbey, Glastonbury Tor, Chalice Well and the Holy Thorn on Wearyall Hill. The Abbey is open every day except Christmas Day, and has a picnic area. All the attractions at Glastonbury are within a short walk of each other, although people need to be reasonably fit to climb the Tor.

Glastonbury Music Festival takes place at the end of June, Glastonbury Tor Fair on the second Monday in September, and Glastonbury Carnival is usually the second week in November.

Exact dates should be checked with the Tourist Information Centre.

NEAREST MAIN TOURIST INFORMATION CENTRE
The Tribunal, 9 High Street, Glastonbury, Somerset, BA6 9DP.
Tel: 01458 832954/ 832949

OTHER FAIRY DWELLING PLACES

There is a strong tradition in Britain of encounters with fairy folk. These were just as real as modern encounters with extraterrestrials are to witnesses today. Is there a connection? Fairies were said to live in toadstools which bear a symbolic resemblance to dome-shaped UFOs.

Harrow Hill in West Sussex, two miles east of the village of Burpham, is crowned with a small prehistoric fort. The hill was believed to be the last place in England inhabited by fairies. There is evidence that the hill was a Neolithic flint mine.

The mountain of Freni-Fawr near Crymch in Dyfed is a gateway to fairyland according to tradition. A boy tending sheep was beckoned by a group of fairies who persuaded him to dance with them. He found himself in fairyland, but transgressed and was transported back to the cold mountainside.

Tomnahurich Hill, a cemetery beside the A82 near Inverness, is allegedly the home of the Fairy Queen. A story describes how a fiddler fell asleep and woke up in an underground palace. There he played for her until exhausted, later finding himself on the bank of the River Ness. His one night in fairyland was one hundred years here.

MORGAWR THE SEA MONSTER

AN OLD SEA PORT

*F*ALMOUTH BAY is a natural harbour which was developed as a port in 1688 and became the centre for the Mail Packet Service. By 1827 thirty-nine vessels were operating from the port, conveying mail to the Mediterranean countries and the Americas. Falmouth went into a decline when steam replaced sail, and the service was transferred to Southampton. In recent years, the coast in and around Falmouth has been the location for sightings of a sea monster.

SIGHTINGS

Reported sightings increased from the mid-1970s. In 1975 local journalist Noel Wain gave the monster the name 'Morgawr', Cornish for 'sea giant'.

In September that year, a Mrs Scott and a Mr Riley were on Pendennis Point at the mouth of the bay when they saw something strange in the water. They described it as a 'lumpy creature', covered in bristles, with a pair of stumpy horns on its head. As they watched, the creature sank beneath the waves, reappearing momentarily with a conger eel in its jaws.

The monster received wider publicity on 5 March 1976 when

the *Falmouth Packet* published two photographs supposedly depicting the beast. They had been taken during the first half of February. A covering letter was signed 'Mary F.', but was not accompanied by an address. 'Mary' said the creature was between 15 and 18 feet long, then added: 'It looked like an elephant waving its trunk, but the trunk was a long neck with a small head on the end, like a snake's head. It had humps on the back which moved in a funny way. The colour was black or very dark brown, and the skin seemed to be like a sealion's.'

Anomaly researchers Janet and Colin Bord examined copies of the prints and found them convincing. But critics pointed out that the beast looked top-heavy and therefore very odd. More of its body projected out of the water than would be possible if it was a real creature.

Central to many of the sightings around Falmouth was a colourful 'wizard' called Anthony 'Doc' Shiels. He claimed to have seen something in the water on several occasions. On 4 July 1976 he was on Greeb beach with his wife Christine and their four children. Shiels kept getting a glimpse of something in the estuary. His children saw it next and then his wife, who described it as 'a large, dark, long-necked, hump-backed beast moving slowly through the water'.

Shiels' second stroke of luck occurred on 17 November. David Clarke, editor of *Cornish Life* magazine, had taken him to Parson's Beach, Mawnan, for photographs to be included in a feature. According to the two men, their attention was drawn towards a 'small dark head' poking out of the water; it came within 70 to 80 feet of the rocky beach. Clarke afterwards wrote: '. . . the greenish black head was supported on a long arched neck, more slender than that of a seal . . .' The head was rounded with a "blunt" nose and on top of the head were two small rounded "buds" . . . at one point a gently rounded black body broke the surface. . . .'

The beast was about 15 feet long with two small stalks or horns on its head. Both men carried cameras, but, amazingly, neither of them was able to produce a decent shot. Shiels' pocket camera was inadequate for the job, and Clarke's 35mm camera fitted with a telephoto lens allegedly malfunctioned and produced a triple exposure of the 'animal'. All this made good copy.

STRANGE

During 1991 and 1992 the American magazine *Strange* published a series of articles which linked Anthony Shiels' and Mary F.'s pictures with several other photographs of alleged water monsters, including two shots taken at Loch Ness. The authors claimed that all of these had been hoaxed by Shiels. A friend of his, Michael McCormick, claimed he had assisted the 'wizard' in faking some of them by attaching a plasticine monster to a sheet of glass, holding it in front of a watery background, then taking a photograph. In convoluted replies Shiels admitted this, but claimed they were experiments to discover how 'Mary F.' might have manufactured her pictures. All in all, it seemed very damning.

OTHER SIGHTINGS IN THE AREA

Despite the grave doubts about the Shiels-associated pictures, there have been other sightings in the area around Falmouth and out at sea.

The *West Briton* discovered in its archives a report which was published in the late nineteenth century and concerned the capture of a sea serpent in Gerrans Bay, off the modern A3078. A Mr Botisto wrote:

> Two of our fishermen were afloat overhauling our crab pots, about four to five hundred yards from the shore when they discovered the serpent coiled about their floating cork [buoy]. Upon their approach it lifted its head and showed signs of defiance, upon which they struck it forcibly with an oar. They pursued it bringing it ashore for exhibition, soon after which it was killed on the rocks and cast into the sea.

Shiels, either for serious intent or merely for publicity purposes, organized some monster-raising experiments on Parson's Beach. These involved young naked witches, including his own daughters. After one ritual on May Eve 1976, two London bankers saw something on the morning of 4 May.

Tony Rogers and John Chambers were fishing near the mouth

of the Helford River, below Mawnan church. According to Rogers, 'Suddenly, something rose out of the water, about 150 or 200 yards away. It was greeny grey and appeared to have humps. Another smaller one appeared. They were visible for about ten seconds and looked straight at us.' Chambers failed to see the smaller creature.

On Friday, 13 May 1977, Mr and Mrs Arthur Wood of Plymstock were taking an early morning stroll along Pendennis Point when they had a double experience. In the sky they observed a bright ball of orange and green fire. Just half an hour later they saw heading out to sea a creature which they could not identify.

In his book *Strange Mysteries of Time and Space* (now out of print), Harold T. Wilkins recorded his experience at Looe, 30 miles to the east of Falmouth. At 11.30 on 5 July 1949,

Myself and another man saw two remarkable saurians 19–20 feet long, with bottle-green heads, one behind the other, their middle parts under the water of the tidal creek of East Looe, Cornwall, apparently chasing a shoal of fish up the creek. What was amazing were their dorsal parts: ridged, serrated, and like the old Chinese pictures of dragons. Gulls swooped down towards the one in the rear, which had a large piece of orange peel on his dorsal parts. These monsters – and two of us saw them – resembled the plesiosaurus of Mesozoic times.

Fifteen miles south of Falmouth is the aptly named Lizard Point. One morning in July 1976 John Cock of Redruth and George Vinnecombe of Falmouth were fishing 25 miles off the coast at Lizard. Vinnecombe spotted what he thought at first was an upturned boat in the water. When he alerted his friend, who came up on deck, they realized that it was a living creature.

The men were experienced fishermen and used to all sorts of whales, but this was something they had never seen before. They closed down the engine and drifted to within 20–30 feet of the beast in clear conditions.

Vinnecombe said it had a back like corrugated iron, and resembled a prehistoric monster. Suddenly it raised its head, like that of an enormous seal, before slowly disappearing beneath the waves. The thing was about 15 feet across, and black and grey in colour.

THE MAWNAN OWL MAN

The village of Mawnan is just three miles south of Falmouth. Above a steep, wooded bank near the Helford River where people have observed Morgawr is Mawnan church, which is actually built inside a prehistoric earthwork. Here, according to local newspapers and Anthony Shiels, is where tourists have been confronted by a terrifying creature.

On 17 April 1976, twelve-year-old June Melling and her nine-year-old sister, Vicky, claimed they saw a creature the size of a man, covered in feathers, hovering over the church tower. Fourteen-year-olds Sally Chapman and Barbara Perry were camping in the trees when at around 10 p.m. they heard a hissing sound. Twenty yards away they saw a man-like figure with pointed ears and glowing red eyes, covered in grey feathers. They thought it was someone dressed up for a joke until it suddenly rose up into the air. As it did so, they noticed it had pincer-like feet. Jane Greenwood of Southport wrote to the *Falmouth Packet* and told them of her sighting with her sister. They too saw the creature in the trees and said its legs 'bent backwards like a bird's'. It then flew straight upwards.

MOTHMAN

Falmouth's Owl Man is reminiscent of a similar creature seen in West Virginia during the late 1960s. Dubbed 'Mothman' it spawned a book by John Keel called *The Mothman Prophecies*. Witnesses described a grey-winged being, as tall as a man and with glowing red eyes. Apparently it didn't flap its wings when it flew!

There were no more reported sightings until June 1978 when a sixteen-year-old girl witnessed 'a monster, like a devil, flying up through the trees near old Mawnan church'. Three young French girls were also frightened near the church by something 'very big, like a great big furry bird'.

As Shiels was connected with many of the Owl Man sightings, one wonders at their true source. However, it is interesting that all of the witnesses to this phenomenon are young females.

LEYS

Researchers Janet and Colin Bord visited Mawnan and later discovered that the church is aligned with three leys:

1. Nare Point (SW 800251), Mawnan church (SW 788272), Mabe church (SW 767325) and Stithians church (SW 731371) – a total of eight and a half miles.
2. Mawnan church (SW 788272), St Anthony church (SW 783257), the Three Brothers of Grugwith (SW 762198) and a tumulus on Arrowan Common (SW 754176) – a total of six and a half miles.
3. Mawnan church (SW 788272), Manaccan church (SW 764250), an earthwork at St Martin-in-Meneage (SW 750238) and a tumulus on Goonhilly Downs (SW 725215) – a total of five and a half miles.

The Bords plotted the alignments on Ordnance Survey map 203, 1: 50000.

How to Find Falmouth

From Exeter take the A30 through Okehampton and Launceston, over Bodmin Moor and past the town of Bodmin. At the junction marked Truro take the left turning on to the A3076, then the A39 south to Penryn and finally Falmouth.
 Consult Ordnance Survey map 204.

NEAREST MAIN TOURIST INFORMATION CENTRE
28 Killigrew Street, Falmouth, Cornwall, TR11 3PN.
Tel: 01326 312300.

OTHER SEA MONSTERS SIGHTED OFF THE ENGLISH COAST

There have been sightings of sea monsters elsewhere on the English coast, particularly on the east side.

One summer in the late 1930s, at Trusthorpe in Lincolnshire, a boy on holiday walking along the sea wall described how he had seen 'a huge snake-like body' partially submerged four hundred yards off the beach. In October 1966 at nearby Chapel St Leonards a woman walking on the beach saw a serpent head and six or seven pointed humps in the sea one hundred yards away.

Sightings have been made off Humberside too. In the late 1930s a woman living at Skiffing near Easington was relaxing on the beach when suddenly she saw a huge creature rise out of the sea. 'It was of a green colour, with a flat head, protruding eyes, and a long flat mouth which opened and shut as it breathed. It was a great length and moved along with a humped glide.'

A couple were sitting on mud cliffs at Hilston in August 1945 when they were surprised by 'a creature with a head and four or five rounded humps each of which was leaving a wake. It was moving rapidly but quite silently along shore northwards in face of a northerly wind.'

A coastguard at Filey Brigg saw a sea monster in 1934. He said it was around thirty feet long and had eyes which shone 'like torchlights'.

South-East England

THE HIGHGATE VAMPIRE

ON THE EDGE OF THE ABYSS

THERE IS SOMETHING about cemeteries that attracts certain of us – a combination of things that cannot be found anywhere else. They possess a melancholy atmosphere which heightens our sense of spirituality and isolates us from the noise and bustle of the outside world, even when that world is just beyond a high brick wall.

Tree-lined paths and avenues draw us past the regiments of the dead. Their names and epitaphs carved in stone are sometimes clear, at other times indecipherable, but always fascinating to the cemetery voyeur. As we slowly walk this place of the dead and try to imagine what lives they led, inwardly we hold our breath. For it is here, in the cemetery, that we stand on the edge of the abyss. Is there an afterlife, or is there nothing but a memory left in the minds of the living?

No burial ground nurtures such emotions more than Highgate Cemetery in north London (see photograph 8 opposite page 168). Its overgrown paths, ivy-clad monuments and funereal buildings resemble the film set of a Gothic drama. Here human eccentricity in abundance joins forces with nature's own macabre hand to create a place of both peace and dread. It is not surprising, then, that in the 1970s the legend of a vampire living in the cemetery emerged into the cold light of day.

THE LEGEND EMERGES

Highgate Cemetery was founded in 1836 when Stephen Geary of the London Cemetery Company purchased 17 acres of hillside land overlooking London. The company's landscape gardener transformed the area into a place of peace and beauty, creating winding paths and planting shrubs and trees. It received much critical acclaim, but problems arose at the start of the First World War.

Both world wars robbed the cemetery of labour, and increased wages made it difficult to employ enough staff even when they were available. On top of that the number of saleable plots was inevitably reduced and in any case cremation was becoming more popular. After years of neglect and vandalization, the cemetery was closed to the public in 1975.

There was much local concern, and a group called the Friends of Highgate Cemetery was set up. A mammoth task confronted the volunteers. They spent several years clearing the dense over-growth, cutting down superfluous trees, replanting elsewhere, and generally tidying up without losing the atmosphere of the place. From all this previous dereliction emerged the Highgate vampire.

Rumours of a vampire living in the cemetery gained substance in 1970, and culminated in a mass vampire hunt on the night of Friday, 13 March. Like a scene from a *Hammer* horror film, a crowd of a hundred or so, some protected with crucifixes and sharpened stakes, rampaged through the tree-lined avenues carrying torches. They were unsuccessful.

MR FARRANT AND MR BLOOD

The hunt followed a television interview with a Mr David Farrant, who later teamed up with an Essex schoolteacher aptly named Alan Blood. In a front page story published the following day by the London *Evening News*, Mr Blood speculated that the crowd of people had driven the vampire from the cemetery – although many of them came away frightened, and some said they had seen something 'crawling in the dark'. Mr Blood planned to wait for the Satan-creature at dawn to discover its lair.

The *Evening News* went on to report that a cine club had admitted using the cemetery to film scenes for a feature called *Vampires at Night*, which it was thought might have started the rumours. But David Farrant disagreed. He claimed that on four occasions he had seen a dark, human-like shape, about eight foot tall, gliding over the vaults.

It was 30 September before the media took an interest again. This time it was the *Daily Mail* which reported that Farrant was being charged with entering enclosed premises for an unlawful purpose. The vampire hunter was caught by a police officer 'red-handed', climbing over the wall of the cemetery armed with a wooden cross and a stake. He was released on a technicality, and left the court saying: 'I won't rest until I catch the vampire of Highgate Cemetery'.

Cemetery workers scoffed at the idea of a vampire, and were dismayed at the damage to many of the vaults by 'vandals'. Almost £9,000 worth of damage had been caused by intruders. Graves had been disturbed, lead stolen from coffins and bodies moved. It was reported that three schoolgirls walking through the cemetery had come across the remains of a woman who had been dragged from a tomb. Farrant blamed the desecration on sinister occult groups, whom he thought were also responsible for releasing the vampire ten years earlier.

He remained convinced that the vampire slept by day in the ancient catacombs. 'He has to be destroyed. He is evil,' was his parting remark.

THE INCORRUPTED CORPSE

A story that helped foster the belief in a vampire took root little more than one hundred years before the mass hunt in Highgate Cemetery. It concerned the artist and poet Dante Gabriel Rossetti. When his beloved Lizzie Siddal died he was devastated. As her open coffin lay ready for burial, he placed a book of manuscript poems, written especially for her, between her cheek and her golden-red hair.

As the years passed Rossetti began to regret his action, for the only copies of his early work were buried in Highgate Cemetery.

His literary ambitions were beginning to flower, and he badly needed to recover the lost verses. After a lot of soul-searching he made secret arrangements to have the coffin exhumed.

INCORRUPTED BODIES

Records of Roman Catholic saints contain the largest number of incorruptibles, although every brand of Christianity and other religions boast of bodies that defy decay. But incorruptibility is not confined to the virtuous. Good and bad alike have been discovered, decades after burial, with their bodies and internal organs preserved. Scientific tests have ruled out the use of embalming fluids which leaves explanations ranging from unusual environmental conditions and high levels of radiation to paranormal possibilities.

The arrangements were carried out by a young man called Howell, through whom Rossetti obtained permission from the Home Secretary. On a night early in October 1869 the deed was carried out. Still full of doubts and regrets, Rossetti could not bring himself to attend the exhumation and remained in Howell's home in Fulham, pacing the floor. Present at the graveside were Howell, a solicitor, a Camberwell doctor and some workmen. The receipted bill of two guineas paid for the work is still in existence.

Lanterns and a small fire lit the eerie scene as the coffin was opened. Howell delivered the manuscript to Rossetti and informed him that Lizzie's hair retained its original colour and that her beauty had not been ravaged by the passage of time. Did Howell invent this to make the deed easier for Rossetti to bare, or was it true? If so, one can see how a belief in vampires in the cemetery might have arisen. The dead rot, while the undead remain pristine until a stake is driven through their heart.

How to Find Highgate Cemetery

The west and east portions of the cemetery are divided by Swains Lane. If travelling by Tube, take the Northern Line and get off at Archway. Walk up Highgate Hill, then at the junction with

Highgate High Street turn left into Waterlow Park. Follow the path through the park, which comes out on Swains Lane at the entrance to the cemetery.

Consult the A–Z London Street Atlas.

TIMES OF OPENING
The Eastern Cemetery, where the tomb of Karl Marx lies, is open April – October, 10 a.m. (11 a.m. weekends) – 5 p.m, and November – March, 10/11 a.m. – 4 p.m.

The Western Cemetery, the one featured here, is open for guided tours only. During the summer tours start on weekdays at noon, 2 p.m. and 4 p.m. and at weekends on the hour, 11 a.m. – 4 p.m. There are no weekday tours in December, January or February. Tours for large groups must be arranged in advance. *Tel: 0181-340 1834* for more information.

OTHER VAMPIRE HAUNTS

The vampire legend is built around the belief that the life force exists in blood. A corpse of the undead could be animated by drinking the blood of the living. When sheep were discovered drained of blood, it was thought by some to be the work of a vampire.

In May 1810 something was attacking sheep around Ennerdale Bridge in Cumbria. Throughout May, seven or eight sheep were killed almost every night. They were not eaten or even savaged, but their attacker bit into the jugular vein and sucked out the blood. The cause was never discovered.

During November and December 1905 dozens of sheep were found dead around Badminton in Gloucestershire and Gravesend in Kent. Sergeant Carter of the Gloucestershire Police commented: 'I can say definitely it is impossible for it to be the work of a dog. Dogs are not vampires, and do not suck the blood of a sheep, and leave the flesh almost untouched.'

Sheep are still mysteriously dying in this way. I investigated a case at a farm near Rhyader in mid-Wales. During August and October 1988 thirty-five sheep were discovered dead or dying. The only marks on them were puncture wounds through which blood had been extracted. Locals saw and heard nothing.

THE HAUNTED TOWERS

A LONG AND BLOODY HISTORY

ONE THEORY TO EXPLAIN GHOSTS is that they are images implanted in the environment during a period of intense emotional outbursts. An electromagnetic impression might be left in this way during a murder, terrible accident or battle, and these recordings could be accidentally triggered by someone who is psychic entering such an environment. What would be observed is a hologram, a replay of an earlier scene. Sometimes the effect would be purely auditory, other times purely visual, and occasionally, though more rarely, both.

If this hypothesis holds true, there is no better example in operation than the Tower of London. For almost a thousand years its walls have soaked up the sight and sound of torture, murder, execution, suicide and misery. If ever any place on Earth should be haunted, then it is the Tower. There have been scores of well-attested sightings. The Tower of London is in fact a collection of several buildings surrounded by battlements, and each part of it has produced anomalous phenomena over the years.

THE WHITE TOWER

This is the massive keep at the heart of the Tower of London. In the torture chamber of the White Tower, Anne Askew's body was almost torn apart on the rack. Is it her agonized screams which have been heard echoing off its walls? Yeoman Warder Geoffrey Abbot told psychic investigator Peter Underwood of several instances when night patrols had heard screams through the White Tower's heavy doors. Some soldiers reported seeing the shadow of a huge axe spread across Tower Green.

Mrs Jerrad Tickell, a Vice-President of the Society for Psychical Research, recorded a strange phenomenon witnessed by an officer in 1954. The man watched as something which resembled smoke emerged from one of the old cannons outside the White Tower. The 'smoke' hovered, formed into a cube, then moved along some railings towards the startled officer. He called a nearby sentry, and they both watched as the 'smoke' dangled off some steps before disappearing.

(Photograph 9 opposite page 169 shows the White Tower.)

THE MARTIN TOWER

The ghost of Anne Boleyn has been seen in an upper room of the Martin Tower, where she was held prisoner for a while. Until 1834 zoo animals were kept at the Tower, which perhaps explains why the apparition of a huge bear was encountered near a door of the Martin Tower in 1815. As the 'creature' advanced towards the witness he thrust at it with his bayonet, but the blade went straight through and struck the door. The poor man never recovered from the shock, and two days later he collapsed and died.

A most curious phenomenon was witnessed in the Martin Tower in 1817 by Edmund Lenthal Swifte, Keeper of the Crown Jewels, and his wife. While they were eating one evening they saw a cylindrical object like a glass tube materialize over the dinner table. As the object moved slowly around the table it was seen to contain two dense 'liquids' of white and pale blue, which incessantly mingled and then separated. Then it touched Mrs Swifte, who screamed. At this her husband picked up a chair and struck out at the manifestation, which instantly disappeared.

At either side of Martin Tower is Northumberland's Walk, named after the 9th Earl of Northumberland who was confined there. Towards the end of the nineteenth century many Warders claimed to have seen his ghost taking a stroll.

THE BLOODY TOWER

This Tower earned its name through the number of murders which have allegedly been carried out within its walls. An earlier Earl of Northumberland was reputed to have been murdered there, and his ghost has often been seen. Most infamous of all is the fifteenth-century murder of the two young princes at the behest of their uncle the Duke of Gloucester, later King Richard III. The brothers have been sighted, walking hand in hand, as a reminder of this hideous crime. But there are other apparitions too.

In the late 1920s a Guardsman on night duty was startled when a white form rose up before him. Although it was indistinct, he interpreted the phenomenon as the figure of a headless woman. In panic he thrust his bayonet through it, when it vanished. But in 1933 another Guardsmen saw the same apparition, which he too thought resembled a headless woman.

A Guards officer training for the Olympic Games experienced a horrible atmosphere near the Bloody Tower archway and was completely overcome by it. Two sentries patrolling beneath the archway in 1978 encountered a strong presence. Suddenly the

---

GHOSTLY EXPLANATIONS

There are several theories to explain the sightings of apparitions:

- Where ghosts are apparently unaware of percipients, it is thought they could be a recording in the environment, triggered off by individuals with psychic abilities.
- Where apparitions react to percipients they may be spirits trapped on Earth, unable to reach the afterlife.
- Contact by spirits through mediums or automatic writing poses another explanation. Although many of the communications convey accurate information, some of it is usually blatantly wrong. Does this mean that intelligences from *elsewhere* are capable of masquerading as spirits?

hair on the back of their necks bristled as an icy blast came out of the archway and blew their capes around their faces. The wind stopped instantly.

Ghosts often appear initially as normal flesh-and-blood people. In 1970 a tourist visiting the Bloody Tower observed a woman with long hair standing by a window. She wore an ankle-length black velvet dress, a white cap and a large gold medallion around her neck. As the visitor was thinking it was someone wearing period costume, the 'woman' started to fade and finally disappeared. Intrigued, the visitor returned a few weeks later and was astounded to observe the same phenomenon again, in exactly the same place!

THE QUEEN'S HOUSE

It was here that Guy Fawkes and his fellow conspirators in the Gunpowder Plot of 1605, who made an attempt to blow up the houses of Parliament, were persuaded to confess. Witnesses claim to have heard screams and the grinding sound of implements of torture. There is a Grey Lady perceived only by women, and a figure in medieval dress has been seen drifting along an upper corridor. Loud footsteps have been heard ascending a stairway at the rear of the building.

An American guest staying in the Queen's House reported hearing 'religious chanting'. At the time she assumed that the faint music and voices were coming from a radio, but when she made enquiries this appeared not to be the explanation. Apparently identical sounds had been decribed by a resident.

According to Yeoman Warder Geoffrey Abbot, there is a room adjoining the one in which Anne Boleyn passed her final days which has a very unpleasant and menacing atmosphere. Witnesses have described a peculiar perfume, and of waking up feeling suffocated. Anne Boleyn herself has been spotted leaving the Queen's House and gliding towards Tower Green, where she was executed on 19 May 1536. Elsewhere in the Tower, according to Lady Biddolph in 1899, a woman wearing a red carnation was observed leaning out of a window. The description fitted that of Anne Boleyn.

Sentries have suffered the wrath of their senior officers because of ghosts! A member of the 60th Rifles watched a white figure materialize in a doorway one evening in 1864. He stabbed at it, but of course that was a useless gesture; and realizing what he was confronted with, the guard fainted. He was discovered unconscious by the Captain of the Guard, who put him on a charge for sleeping on duty. At the court martial he told his senior officers what had happened, and several other guards came forward to say they too had seen the apparition. The court acquitted him. Another sentry was acquitted from a charge of deserting his post after he fled upon seeing the figure of a headless woman walking towards Tower Green.

ONE MAN'S EXPERIENCES

John Howden, a young soldier serving with the 2nd Battalion of Scots Guards, had several experiences at the Tower. The first happened one night in January 1966 whilst he was on guard near Traitor's Gate.

He distinctly heard the sound of marching feet. They seemed to be coming through the Tower archway, complete with the sharp crack made by boot studs making contact with the cobblestones. Soldiers were not allowed to wear studded boots after 10 p.m. He approached the archway, raised his bayonet and called out a challenge. Sweating with fear, he walked through the archway, but there was no one about – not even the sentry at No. 1 Post, who should have been standing outside the oak door leading into the Bloody Tower. Then that sentry appeared. He too had heard the sounds, and had gone as far as Tower Green to investigate.

It was John's turn for guard duty outside the Bloody Tower when he had his second experience, during the summer of 1967. His duty was from 1 to 3 a.m., during which time he would patrol as far as Tower Green. On one of these excursions, John noticed a very bright, shimmering light in one of the windows of the White Tower. He stood staring at it for ten minutes, then returned to his post without reporting the matter. Twenty minutes later he went back to the White Tower and found it in darkness. As he walked away he glanced up again and the light had returned – indeed, it was moving from window to window and he could make out the outline of a figure, which moved away as if going to the other side of the Tower. John walked around to the other side, but there was no sign of it, and so he resumed his guard duty. John later learned that other soldiers had also witnessed the phenomenon, and it was thought to be the ghost of Anne Boleyn.

ELSEWHERE IN THE TOWER

In 1973 occupants residing in the Constable Tower experienced a strong 'horsey' smell followed by a 'presence'. It was an odour composed of leather and horse sweat.

Lady Jane Grey was executed at the Tower in 1554 with her husband. She had been Queen of England for only three weeks, and was just sixteen years of age. On 12 February 1957, her ghost was seen in the Tower. The witness was a young Welsh Guardsman called Johns. It was a cold, wintry early morning when a rattling drew his attention towards the battlements of Salt Tower. Forty feet above him he saw, silhouetted against the dark sky, a white, shapeless mass. As he looked, the material took on the form of a young woman in period clothing, which he assumed to be Lady Jane Grey. Another guard appeared, by which time the figure had gone. But as Johns pointed, it came back and they both saw it.

There is a curious story connected with the Chapel of St Peter ad Vincula, involving an officer of the Guard who investigated a light shining through its windows. He was astounded by what he saw. Moving along the aisle was a procession of medieval knights and ladies, led by a woman whose face and costume resembled those of Anne Boleyn. Suddenly the tableau vanished like a light being switched off.

Many other sightings of ghosts, including that of Henry VI, have been reported from other parts of the Tower of London. It must rank as one of Britain's most haunted places.

How to Find the Tower of London

The Tower of London is situated on the River Thames by Tower Bridge. Tower Hill Tube station (Circle and District Line) is nearby.

Aside from its numerous ghosts, the Tower also houses the Crown Jewels which are on public exhibition. Free tours of the Tower by Yeoman Warders take place during the day except in bad weather. The Tower is open Monday – Saturday, 9 a.m. – 6 p.m. and Sunday, 10 a.m. – 6 p.m.

Consult the A–Z London Street Atlas.

NEAREST MAIN TOURIST INFORMATION CENTRE
In this instance it is best to contact the information centre inside the Tower. *Tel: 0171-222 7110.*

OTHER HAUNTED PLACES IN LONDON

Whole books have been written about the haunted places in and around London. There is only room here to give a flavour of a few of them.

A remarkable photograph was taken in 1966 of the Tulip Staircase in the Queen's House at the National Maritime Museum, Greenwich. The staircase was designed and constructed by Inigo Jones in 1629. The picture, taken by the Revd Hardy and his wife from British Columbia, shows the shadowy outline of two figures climbing the stairs. One is hooded and their hands can clearly be seen on the rail.

The Theatre Royal in Drury Lane is said to be haunted by two spectres. One has been described wearing a powdered wig and three cornered hat and is thought to be linked to a skeleton discovered with a dagger through its ribs during alterations in 1848. The other is thought to be the spirit of music hall star Dan Leno.

Westminster Abbey is said to have been built on a pagan site. It boasts several ghosts including a soldier seen near the Tomb of the Unknown Warrior and a Benedictine monk. This latter appeared in 1932 to a group of three people who heard it speak in Elizabethan English. He told them he had been killed at the time of Henry VIII.

HAUNTED DOVER CASTLE

REDOLENT WITH HISTORY

FROM SEA OR LAND, Dover Castle is a very impressive sight. The current building was constructed mainly in the twelfth and thirteenth centuries, but there have been fortifications on the site from prehistoric times. Dover has been of primary defence importance from Roman times to the Second World War, for a very good reason. The castle overlooks an important harbour that opens up to the shortest sea route to mainland Europe. France, which can be seen from the White Cliffs on a clear day, is just 21 miles away.

Julius Caesar landed close to here to occupy England in the first-century BC. Later, the Angles, Jutes and Saxons used Dover as a bridgehead. At the time of the Norman invasion in 1066 the Bishop of Bayeux landed with the prefabricated parts for a castle. In 1588 ships of the Spanish Armada were wrecked on the nearby Goodwin Sands. Cromwell seized it during the Civil War in the seventeenth century, and it was considerably fortified against the threat of an invasion by Napoleon in the early 1800s. In more recent times Dover was of prime importance during both world wars.

Buried beneath all these bloody layers of history, Dover Castle is just the sort of place to possess the necessary background and environment for supernatural phenomena.

GHOSTS OF DOVER CASTLE

In the castle grounds is the restored church of St Mary-in-Castro (see photograph 10 opposite page 169), while a Roman lighthouse is situated at the west end. In this latter place the ghost of a Roman soldier and a hooded monk have been seen. The castle itself is said to be haunted by a drummer boy murdered during the Napoleonic Wars. Staff have witnessed apparitions wearing the apparel of the 1600s, principally a pikeman and a figure in Royalist garb. Investigators believe the castle is haunted by at least six different ghosts.

AN INVESTIGATION

Three overnight vigils have been carried out since 1991 by members of the Thanet Psychic and Paranormal Research Unit and the Association for the Scientific Study of Anomalous Phenomena (ASSAP). Research Co-ordinator Robin Laurance reported on the investigation.

On 12 October 1991 the team assembled at the castle, and at precisely 11.22 p.m. the first incident occurred. Davis Thomas, who was patrolling the passageway leading to the Spur – which extends like an arrowhead away from the Keep – heard a sound like a heavy wooden door slamming shut. At 2.20 a.m. two separate incidents were reported.

The team positioned on the second floor of the Keep heard a loud bang from behind locked doors leading to the west stairwell. Investigation revealed no rational cause, so they relocked the double doors. As they walked away from them the wooden doors were suddenly shaken vigorously for a few seconds.

Two members stationed in the lower St Johns Tower area saw a shadowy figure moving slowly down the stone stairwell at the end of the lower caponier, the covered passage along the ditch. One of them called out to the figure, which turned and moved rapidly back up the stairs. They decided it must have been their fellow investigator John Solley, but when they questioned him later he said he had not walked down the stairs at all during the shift, and at that precise moment he was at the other end of the passageway leading to the Spur.

During the next shift these same two members were to have a further experience. They were in the passageway formerly occupied by Solley when they heard a heavy wooden door being shut twice, at 3.30 a.m. and 4.40 a.m. This was recorded on audiotape. Other members heard doors slamming in different parts of the castle, but the most significant event occurred at 5.20 a.m.

Another team positioned on the second floor of the Keep suddenly experienced the double doors shaking vigorously, this time for approximately six seconds. Thankfully, a video camera trained on the doors recorded the event. A thorough and immediate check was made, but fraud was ruled out.

During the second vigil, on 30 November 1991, a tape recorder was discovered switched off in the mural gallery of the Keep. Before it was switched off the sounds of it being interfered with were recorded. In this same location a strong smell of perfume was detected by the team, and later, in the basement area of the Keep, two loud thuds were heard. At the third vigil, however, on 9 May 1992, no paranormal phenomena were recorded.

THE PHANTOM GHOST SHIP OF THE GOODWIN SANDS

A few miles to the east of Dover Castle lie the Goodwin Sands. This was a treacherous place for shipping with a dozen ships coming aground every year. It was inevitable then that there should be tales of a ghost ship. This was the *Lady Luvibund* which was wrecked on St Valentine's Day 1748, when the first mate deliberately ran it aground. He was taking revenge on the captain who had married the girl he secretly loved. Since then the ship has been encountered by other vessels every fifty years – according to some authors.

The story has appeared in dozens of books of true marine mysteries, *but the ship never existed*! Checks confirmed that no ship of that name was ever listed, and that the story was relatively modern.

Modern Ghosts

Beneath Dover Castle exist miles of underground tunnels. These were first excavated in Napoleonic times, but were extended during World War II for military operations. Since they were recently opened to the public there have been a number of ghostly encounters. Tour guide Leslie Simpson vividly remembers an incident while in the underground Defence Telecommunications Network Station, called 'Hellfire Corner'.

He was talking to a group of people in the Repeater Station when he noticed the odd behaviour of a woman. She was looking away from the group and suddenly grew alarmed then fell. She told Leslie that she had been watching a man in naval uniform tinkering with the equipment. He had then turned and walked towards her, right through the crowd. As he passed through her she slipped, before seeing him disappear through the exit. Later that same day, Leslie heard a strange noise coming from an adjacent room. It was a weird mechanical whining sound, intermixed with an animal noise.

A few months later an Italian tourist saw the same apparition, but when he asked Leslie who the 'man' was, neither the guide nor the other tourists could see anyone.

Another guide, Karen Mennie, also observed the odd reaction of a couple in the Repeater Station one summer's day in 1993. She noticed a father and daughter standing slightly away from the rest of the group. The girl appeared to be in communication with somebody who was not there, and her father was looking on with interest. Afterwards he told Karen what had happened. Apparently they had unknowingly been in conversation with a ghost! He had said his name was 'Bill Billings' and that he had been a Postal Telecommunications Officer from Canterbury, killed whilst assembling one of the 'Amplifier Racks' during World War II. Efforts to trace relatives of 'Bill Billings' met with failure. Neither was he listed as being stationed at the castle, although it was admitted that castle records were incomplete.

How to Find Dover Castle

Take the M2 from Rochester, then the A2 through Canterbury to Dover.

The castle is owned by English Heritage and open to the public. In exceptional circumstances the staff will consider investigation by recognized organizations.

Consult Ordnance Survey map 179.

NEAREST MAIN TOURIST INFORMATION CENTRE
Townwall Street, Dover, Kent, CT16 1JR. *Tel: 01304 205108.*

OTHER HAUNTED ENGLISH CASTLES

Lindisfarne Castle on Holy Island in Northumberland, was built on high rocks around 1550. It is said to be haunted by St Cuthbert who came there in A.D. 664. In modern times witnesses have described seeing a Cromwellian soldier in the castle. Sir Edwin Lutyens converted the castle into a home in 1903, and it is now owned by the National Trust.

There was once a priory on the island which has produced many sightings of ghost monks. An account was published in 1968 of the regular appearance of a monk to one of the choir boys. He talked of 'a tall man, a nice man' who often disappeared through a wall. The apparition, who wore a browny-black gown tied with a rope, had his hair cut away in a curious half-moon shape. Research by the Revd A. W. Jackson found that this tonsure was characteristic of Celtic monasteries.

Corfe Castle near Purbeck in Dorset, pictured on the cover of this book, has a long bloody history. In 978 King Edward was murdered by his stepmother who wanted her son Ethelred crowned. According to the tale, the body was hidden in a well where a mysterious light glowed above it.

King John made the castle a royal residence in the thirteenth century and here he imprisoned and starved to death twenty-two French noblemen. Horrors were also visited on the castle during the Civil War in the 1640s when it was blown up by Parliamentarians. One of the phantom figures seen often near the castle is that of a headless woman. In 1976 a group of three visitors observed her at the foot of the castle hill.

THE LONG MAN OF WILMINGTON AND THE SECRET LANDSCAPE

POWER CENTRES ON THE DOWNS?

THERE ARE SEVERAL GIANT IMAGES of men and animals cut into the chalk hills of southern England. Ranking with the Long Man of Wilmington is the Cerne Abbas Giant in Dorset, a club-bearing figure 180 feet long which, with its erect penis, seems to represent a fertility god.

The images were placed there during ancient times, and controversy rages as to their purpose. Were they created by pagan artists who wished to propitiate their deities, or was there an even deeper purpose? Are the locations of more importance than they first appear? Could they be centres of power, connected with earth energies and leys?

Circumstantial evidence indicates that, in the case of the Long Man of Wilmington, that could be so. Psychic experiments carried out in 1987 had some startling results. But the whole area around Wilmington seems to be part of a cohesive whole – a landscape of magic which was manipulated by medieval monks.

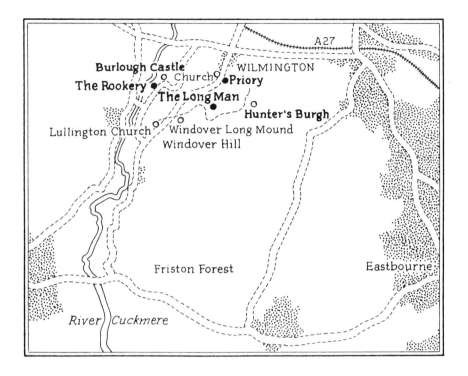

A GIANT SECRET

The Long Man is 240 feet tall, cut into the steep north slope of Windover Hill. It depicts a man with his arms raised, each hand holding what appears to be a pole of some kind. What tourists see today is a restored version of the original (see photograph 11 opposite page 184). The Revd de St Croix bricked in the outline in 1874, subtly changing it. What we now see are 770 kerb stones which were set into the turf in the late 1960s and painted brilliant white. Previously the figure had existed only as depressions in the turf, but it became plainly visible, as if by magic, in the slanting rays of early morning and late evening light. Although it is accepted that the Giant is ancient, references to it date back only as far as 1766.

To the east of the Long Man is Hunter's Burgh, a Neolithic long barrow. Above him is Windover Long Mound, another long barrow. So the Long Man stands sentinel over a secret landscape steeped in paganism and mystery.

WILMINGTON PRIORY

At the foot of the Long Man, about half a mile away on the southern end of Wilmington village, sits Wilmington Priory. Its mother foundation was the Abbey of Grestain, near Honfleur in Normandy. The original medieval building has been restored, with little of its thirteenth- and fourteenth-century construction remaining; but there is a crypt which survives from that time.

The crypt extends as a short underground passage to the nearby church; that too has its pagan associations. In the churchyard stands a giant yew tree, 23 feet in girth and supported by crutches and chains, which dates back a thousand years. At its foot is a curious oblong stone. Did pagan Saxons use this stone for sacrifices?

At the southern end of the crypt there seems to be the beginning of another passageway. Did this lead into Windover Hill? Researchers have pondered over whether the monks created the Long Man, or whether they built the monastery nearby because of Wilmington's strong pagan links. Were they seeking to use its magical powers?

Potsherds found embedded in silt covering the figure offer evidence that it is much older than the thirteenth century. The monks at the Priory were known to practise secret rituals which were hardly Christian, and so it is possible that the latter explanation is nearer the truth.

In 1315 Prior William – who became known as Paganus de Capella – had a chapel built on a mound surrounded by trees; it was called the Rookery. Close by is a place known as Burlough Castle, and the River Cuckmere once meandered past them both. This location is less than a mile from the Long Man. It is thought that the chapel was used for occult rites and was protected from prying eyes by the screen of trees. Burlough Castle itself is a mystery. There is no castle on the low hill, and no evidence has been found that one was ever built. In Sussex folklore, the hill was said to be the headquarters of the fairies. Was Burlough Castle an invisible fairy castle?

Three-quarters of a mile south of Burlough Castle is Lullington church, the smallest church in England – it too is surrounded by trees. There is speculation that the church was built inside a Celtic sacred grove; religious ceremonies took place in clearings within these groves.

THE IDENTITY OF THE LONG MAN

Did the monks interpret the Giant as representing Mercurius, a symbol of alchemists concerned with the unification of opposites? Mercurius is often pictured, arms raised, each hand holding a rod to keep apart adversaries until they can be safely united. The opposites in the minds of the medieval monks were Christianity and paganism. In their eyes, perhaps, the Long Man had achieved unification between them. The figure represented their own dichotomy: they were Christians involved in occult practices.

To more orthodox Christians the figure may have represented Samson, with the staves becoming the pillars that he pulled down on the Philistines. The Giant has also been compared to the Green Man, Hearne the Hunter, Pan and other nature gods.

Whatever the true identity of the Giant, it seems that the monks hoped its power would enrich their lives.

THE GREEN MAN

The Green Man is a complex archetypal figure dating back to pre-history who is still celebrated today in the wealth of pub signs bearing his name.

He is a nature deity in many guises. As Herne the Hunter, he was an antlered woodland being, as Pan he was a horned nature god who Christianity turned into the Devil, and in his most accessible guise he was Robin Hood in his tunic of Lincoln green.

THE CHESSBOARD LANDSCAPE

Researcher Rodney Castleden identifies the Wilmington landscape with a medieval French romance called the *Petit Saint Graal*. In one episode Peredur, the hero, is sent on a quest and comes upon a castle with no inhabitants. Inside is a chessboard on which the pieces are playing by themselves. Peredur takes sides and loses, throwing the board out of the window into a river.

A maiden appears, rebukes him for losing his temper, and sets him a task: he must go to a nearby wood to kill and behead a white hart. This he does, but then a mysterious knight appears and makes off with the head. Peredur has failed again. As a punishment he is sent to a mound beneath which is carved the figure of a man. After Peredur recites a spell, a huge wild black man springs from the mound. The pair do battle and Peredur wins, after which the wild man disappears back into the mound.

Castleden cites Burlough Castle, the River Cuckmere, the grove where Lullington church was built and the barrows near the Long Man – who features graphically in the tale – as the locations mentioned in the romance. Hunter's Burgh would seem to commemorate the hunting of the hart, and Windover Long Mound to be the place from which the wild black man sprung.

Rodney Castleden believes that the story is a cipher for the activities of the cult which practised around Wilmington from the Priory.

THE LEY EXPERIMENT

Earth light researcher Paul Devereux discovered a two-mile-long ley passing through the figure. The nodal points from south to north are a tumulus in Friston Forest, Windover Long Mound, the Long Man, and Wilmington Priory and church.

Dowsers who have operated around Wilmington claim to have detected the energy of the ley. One of them is Kevin Carlyon, who decided to set up an experiment to see if leys are capable of carrying thought over great distances. He became convinced that the site contained a ley of positive and negative power that could be channelled for healing and other purposes.

The experiment was carried out on the nights of 4 and 25 October 1986. A number of 'senders' were positioned near the Giant, with 'receivers' based around Britain and in other parts of the world. On each night the senders concentrated their thoughts on five sounds and five objects.

Twelve hundred test forms were sent out. Out of these, 756 were completed and returned. Carlyon claimed some remarkable results. One man, who had entered as a joke, got eight of the ten items not only right but also in the correct order. Many more supplied the right answers, but in the wrong order. Some of those who had none right obtained the same wrong answers as their partners. The experiments were interesting enough for two universities to take an interest in further analysis of the results.

THE OLD MAN RETURNS

Whilst travelling from Brighton to Eastbourne in the early hours of Saturday 3 December 1994, Brian Trotter and his passenger drove straight into a mystery. They had just passed Selmston when they noticed a brilliant white light in the direction of the Long Man. The pair thought that someone must have illuminated the figure for Christmas and decided to take a closer look. They turned into the village of Milton Street and followed a track which led to an open field, half a mile away from the glowing figure.

The figure was more brightly lit than neon. The luminescense twinkled and from the valley below issued a softer yellowish light. The witnesses described it to me as 'awe inspiring'. Realising that their original explanation could not adequately account for the strange phenomenon, the couple became afraid and drove off.

Returning in daylight to Milton Street, they discovered that a fold in the hill prevented them from seeing the whole figure. What is more, they remembered seeing the Long Man with his feet pointing *downwards* although the feet are actually positioned sideways. The pair had apparently seen the Long Man before its restoration in 1874, when the feet did indeed point downhill.

How to Find the Long Man of Wilmington

The village of Wilmington is just a few miles west of Eastbourne off the A27 at the foot of the South Downs. The Giant and the other places are within walking distance for reasonably fit people – footpaths cross Windover Hill to Lullington. Alternatively, most of them can be reached by following the minor road through Wilmington to Lullington. The Benedictine priory is owned by the

Sussex Archaeological Trust.

See the map on page 144 and also consult Ordnance Survey map 199.

NEAREST MAIN TOURIST INFORMATION CENTRE
Cornfield Road, Eastbourne, East Sussex, BN21 4QL.
Tel: 01323 411400.

How to Find the Cerne Abbas Giant

To support his argument, Rodney Castleden also cites the Cerne Abbas Giant. It too has an earthwork above its head and an abbey at its feet! For centuries childless couples have made love in the phallus of the Giant, and many claim to have conceived afterwards. Not far from the abbey ruins, St Augustine's Well can be seen. The village of Cerne Abbas is six miles north of Dorchester in Dorset, off the A352.

OTHER CHALK FIGURES

The figure cut into the chalk at Uffington in Oxfordshire is somewhat ambiguous. Is it a horse or a dragon? Below the figure is Dragon Hill, and above it an Iron Age hill fort called Uffington Castle. Tradition has it that St George killed the dragon here, its blood poisoning the grass and laying bare the chalk. Over the years the chalk has been cleaned, perhaps modifying the figure and changing it from a dragon to a horse. It can be reached off the B4507.

Six miles south of Aylesbury in Buckinghamshire, on the steep west facing slope of the Chiltern Hills, is the Whiteleaf Cross. No one knows when the figure was first carved into the chalky hillside, but it is thought that originally it was a phallic symbol which monks later re-shaped. It can be approached up a steep lane from the village of Whiteleaf.

See also the White Horse of Westbury on page 107.

THE MENACE OF NETLEY ABBEY

A DREADFUL WARNING UNHEEDED

MOST SUPERNATURAL PRESENCES seem to be indifferent to mortal observers. Only poltergeists usually interact directly with human beings. But in the ruins of Netley Abbey, near Southampton, witnesses have experienced something hostile.

The abbey was built in the first half of the thirteenth century, under the instructions of Henry III, by monks from a Cistercian abbey across the English Channel in Beaulieu. It supported a thriving religious community until 1536. Then, after the Dissolution of the Monasteries, it was used as a private dwelling. There grew up a legend that buried treasure was hidden on the land, guarded by the entity of a hooded monk. Another story speaks of a secret chamber containing the treasure, and of the remains of a 'renegade nun' bricked up alive.

In the eighteenth century, a man named Walter Taylor owned the property, which he intended to demolish so that he could use the stone for other building purposes. Taylor had a vivid dream in which the keystone of an archway fell on him. He disregarded it, and the work began. When he was killed by a stone falling from a window arch, demolition work stopped and the abbey was left to fall into ruin. No one dared risk the abbey's 'curse' again.

It had been derelict for over two hundred years when the poet and romantic Thomas Gray visited it in 1764. At that time the ruins lay in the midst of dense woodland and must have presented an eerie sight. The ferryman who conveyed Gray across Southampton Water told him that he 'would not for all the world' go near it in the dark for 'there were things seen near it' and 'power of money was hidden there'.

BLIND PETER

The entity experienced by people venturing into the ruins at night became known as 'Blind Peter', although no one knows why. An apparition has been seen hovering over the sacristy – the place where sacred vessels and vestments were kept – and sensed in the form of a hostile presence in the ruins themselves.

MODERN SIGHTINGS

One summer's day in 1970 a local woman called Mrs Neal and her friend decided to conduct some dowsing experiments in the grounds of Abbey House, adjacent to the abbey. After some while the stick began to react violently. Mrs Neal followed the course indicated for several yards before turning to the right.

Ahead of her she saw a tall, slim figure dressed as a monk in a dark brown cloak with a loose-fitting hood which caused a shadow to hide the face. He beckoned twice in a delicate fashion with his right hand, then pointed in the direction of the abbey as if he was trying to convey something to her. While the encounter lasted, Mrs Neal felt as if she was enchanted. Time had no meaning. She could not tell afterwards whether the experience had lasted seconds or minutes, although it must have been the former. Her friend, while sensing a 'potent atmosphere', saw nothing.

In 1981 a couple and their dog camped out in the ruins. They were awakened in the early hours by a sudden drop in temperature and the feeling that 'something' was prowling outside the tent. Even the dog was affected. It growled, and when it was sent outside to investigate ran off.

DOWSING

Dowsing is of medieval origin and is accepted by many scientists today as *fact*. It is the art of finding water, minerals, buried treasure and general information by non-physical means and it can be tried by anyone.

Many dowsers use indicators, usually a forked twig, a pair of bent coat hangers or a pendulum. The indicator will twitch or change direction when the dowser is close to what he is seeking.

See also *Wotton-under-Edge,* page 95, and *Loch Morar*, page 170.

Two nuns visiting the ruins by day experienced a sudden temperature drop near the sacristy and sensed a 'distinct presence' which conveyed hostility to them.

Visit Netley Abbey if you dare!

How to Find Netley Abbey

Netley Abbey is on the east side of Southampton Water. Follow the signs for Netley from Southampton.

Consult Ordnance Survey map 196.

NEAREST MAIN TOURIST INFORMATION CENTRE

Above Bar, Southampton, Hampshire, S09 4XF. *Tel: 01703 221106.*

OTHER HAUNTED ABBEYS

Lacock Abbey near Chippenham in Wiltshire was consecrated as an Augustinian convent in 1232 by Ela, Countess of Salisbury, and came into the possession of the National Trust in 1944. At the time of the Dissolution of the Monasteries, Henry VIII sold the Abbey to the Sharington family. Henry Sharington's daughter wanted to marry John Talbot but her father disapproved – until she threw herself from the tower. Olive was saved by her skirts which filled with air, and Henry granted her wish.

It is believed that Ela and Olive haunt the Abbey. According to ghost hunter Peter Underwood, a friend of his saw a beautiful girl on the drive facing the west front. He took a photograph before approaching the figure which then disappeared. The processed picture showed the Abbey but no girl.

Woburn Abbey in Woburn, Bedfordshire is definitely haunted, according to the thirteenth Duke of Bedford. Members of the family, plus guests like Paul Getty, have witnessed doors opening by themselves and heard inexplicable footsteps. A cleaning lady saw the apparition of a monk, and visitors have recounted seeing a strange 'man' in a top hat. There are rooms with a decidedly sinister atmosphere where guests refuse to sleep, and dogs whimper and howl. In the Sculpture Gallery there is a ghost with a preference for women. Over the years many have attested to being touched by an invisible hand!

WHATEVER HAPPENED TO LUCY LIGHTFOOT?

THE DOG THAT DANCED WITH FAIRIES

THE STORY OF LUCY LIGHTFOOT is intriguing, mysterious, sad and romantic. At the centre of the affair lies St Olave's church in the tiny village of Gatcombe on the Isle of Wight. But the tale has its roots in Palestine too and on the Isles of Scilly. They weave together two stories, and two Lucy Lightfoots – or is it just one?

In Gatcombe church rests a carved oak figure of a crusader called Edward Estur. The church was built by the Estur family, who came across from Normandy in 1290. They had strong links with Norway and named it St Olave's, after the Norwegian saint of that name.

The effigy lies on the north side of the sanctuary in a recess in the thick stone walls. A carved angel sits at the head of the crusader, and his feet rest on a small dog. Tradition has it that the animal comes to life every hundred years on Midsummer's Eve. Then it runs into the woods and dances on its hind legs with the fairy folk, telling them tales of its adventures in the Holy Land – adventures which ended in tragedy.

THE CRUSADER AND THE FARMER'S DAUGHTER

Edward Estur joined the army of Peter I, King of Cyprus, and fought the Sultan of Egypt along the coast of Syria. It was there that he received his fatal wound: a sword stroke split Edward's helmet, shattering his skull. After four months in a coma he was shipped from Alexandria back to the Isle of Wight. He recovered consciousness, but was badly brain-damaged. Edward lingered for a further few months but then died.

Five centuries later, in the early 1800s, a child was born in the nearby hamlet of Bowcombe who grew into a beautiful young woman. The daughter of a farmer, she was called Lucy Lightfoot. Her good looks, tomboyish nature and skilled horsemanship made her very desirable to the young men in the area. But Lucy's attentions were directed elsewhere.

During her devout worshipping at St Olave's Lucy developed an intense fixation with the effigy of Edward Estur. It went beyond mere fascination and became obsessive. She fell deeply in love with the wooden carving of a man who had died centuries before she was born.

Hardly a day passed without her riding up from Stoney Meadow Farm to visit the effigy. After hitching her horse to the church porch she would spend an hour or so in the company of Edward, gazing into his bland wooden features. He carried a shield and clutched in his right hand a steel misericord, a dagger used by medieval knights to dispatch fallen opponents. The hilt of Edward's misericord was adorned with a chrysoberyl set in an engraved lodestone.

At one point the vicar let his irritation with the bizarre visits spill over. 'Why do you stand so?' He asked her. Still staring at the object of her desires, she replied in a faraway voice that she 'loved to be with him in her thoughts and dreams'. What were her thoughts and were they eventually realized?

St. Olave's, Gatcombe

LUCY LIGHTFOOT VANISHES

Lucy set out on horseback on the morning of 13 June 1831 to visit a friend, Marjorie Braithwaite, who lived a few miles away in Chillerton. On her way there, Lucy rode through Gatcombe and apparently could not resist visiting the church. Witnesses saw her tether her horse to the porch and disappear inside.

Almost at once the most violent storm in the island's history erupted above the village. For two hours rain lashed down, driving crops into the sodden ground. Lightning hit the island, killing cattle and setting fire to buildings. It was a storm of tropical violence. On top of this a total eclipse of the sun took place just after eleven o'clock, plunging the already gloomy island into darkness for forty minutes.

When the storm finally abated the sun returned and normality resumed. A farmer named George Brewster saw Lucy's distressed mare still tethered to the church porch. He went inside the building looking for the young woman, wondering how she had fared in the storm. She was nowhere in sight, and was never seen again.

Despite a large reward offered by her parents, no clue or information emerged as to her fate. Devastated, two years after the loss they sold Stoney Meadow Farm and moved to Stanton Fitzwarren in Wiltshire. The farm was subsequently razed to the ground under mysterious circumstances.

What had happened to Lucy Lightfoot? Had she been murdered and her body hidden? The vicar found no sign of a struggle. What he did find was that the dagger had been torn from the hand of Edward Estur and smashed by some force. Fragments were found on the altar, but the chrysoberyl, like Lucy, had completely vanished.

OTHER MYSTERIOUS DISAPPEARANCES

There are a large number of people who disappear under strange circumstances. Here are two well-known cases:

- On 6 April 1922 twelve-year-old French girl Pauline Picard disappeared. She was found several days later 230 miles away in Cherbourg, suffering amnesia. She disappeared again in May. Four days later, Pauline's headless corpse was found half a mile from her home, her clothes folded neatly nearby. The inquest ruled she had died from exhaustion, her body defaced by predators.
- Frederick Valentich was flying his Cessna over the Bass Strait in Australia on the night of 21 October 1978 when he notified ground control that a long metallic object was circling his aircraft. Then there was a screeching sound, and silence. Extensive searches of the area failed to find a body or any wreckage.

A FURTHER TWIST

The story is fascinating enough as it stands, but it took an even more remarkable turn thirty-four years later. In 1865 the Revd Samuel Trelawney, minister of St Mary's Methodist church on the Isles of Scilly, came across an ancient manuscript. Trelawney was a student of the crusades, and it was during his researches that a document written by Philippe de Mézières, Chancellor to Peter I, came into his hands. He learned from it how Edward Estur had joined Peter's army. The manuscript listed all the volunteers – and their companions. In Edward's case it recorded the name of a woman from the district of Carisbrooke Castle on the Isle of Wight. Her name was Lucy Lightfoot.

According to the manuscript, Lucy was eager to travel with her lover to the Holy Land, but he forbade it because of the dangers. Edward persuaded her to stay in Cyprus, and promised that on their return to England he would marry her.

The manuscript records that Lucy waited three years for Edward before she learned of his death. She sailed for Corsica and married a fisherman called Lionallo Momellino from Terra Vecchia, now Bastia. Despite her loss she settled down to a happy life growing fruit and rearing a large family. She died at an advanced age and was buried in the village church.

Were the two Lucys one and the same person linked by reincarnation? Or were they of the same family line, as seems likely? If so, did the nineteenth-century Lucy Lightfoot carry a genetic memory of her ancestor's love for the crusader? But even so, what happened to the girl in St Olave's church?

Police surgeon Dr Harry Grimshaw speculated along scientific lines to the late rector of St Olave's, the Revd James Evans, a keen folklorist. Dr Grimshaw remarked on the intense magnetism released by the crystals of a lodestone when disintegrated under pressure. Did lighting strike the dagger while Lucy Lightfoot stood near the effigy? Could the resultant intense electromagnetic field, combined with the woman's insane desire to be with Edward Estur, have sent her through a kink in space and time to be with him? Was there only one Lucy Lightfoot after all?

When I spoke to the present rector of St Olave's, the Revd Jonathan Russell, I voiced my reservations about the story. He gave me his thoughts on James Evans, who was responsible for publicizing the case. 'I was lucky enough to talk with him several times before his death a few years ago,' he said. 'The Revd Evans was a delightful Welsh clergyman, very fond of old stories and legends. One of his maxims was that every legend had to start somewhere.'

ALSO NEARBY - HAUNTED PUBS

There are a number of haunted pubs on the Isle of Wight. At the Castle Inn in Newport, a seventeenth-century former coaching inn, a 'whistling ghost' is often heard by staff. Steve and Elizabeth Taylor ran the pub until 1991. Elizabeth was alone in the bar one night when she saw a white shape enter through the door and move across the room. Apart from whistling, the entity often worked the remote control of the television set in the bar, changing channels. The phenomenon also developed a taste for the Taylors' video machine. They watched, astounded, as channels were switched while they were recording. The equipment was checked out, but nothing was found to explain it. According to a psychic, the spirit belongs to a stable lad who hanged himself in the old hayloft in the 1600s.

The Red Lion at Church Place, Freshwater, dates from the twelfth century. The late Ron Legg and his staff often heard heavy footsteps trudging through the building. Bryan and Anita Farrant, who took the pub over, also heard footsteps, and experienced sudden drops in temperature in the upstairs lounge.

Paranormal phenomena can be so convincing that they are indistinguishable from 'reality'. This was the case when the landlord of the Solent Inn in Monkton Street, Ryde, called the police because he believed the pub was being burgled! Chris and Belinda Cocknell were in their bedroom when they heard the noise of furniture being pushed around in the lounge below. They were convinced that someone had broken in, and Chris dialled 999. The noise went on for ten minutes, but when the police arrived nothing had been disturbed. When it happened again, a few weeks later, the couple went down to investigate. Again, nothing was amiss, and all the doors and windows were secure. The pub has a history of haunting. Belinda's parents were the previous owners, and they recorded many incidents including phantom footsteps and voices.

Other haunted pubs include the Plough and Barleycorn in Shanklin, the Partlands Hotel in Ryde, the Sloop Inn at Wootton Bridge, the Bugle Hotel in Newport, and the Duke of York in Cowes.

ALSO NEARBY - THE LONGSTONE OF MOTTISTONE

The 13-foot-tall Longstone stands with its smaller horizontal companion on National Trust property behind Mottistone manor house. Like other standing stones it is thought to have power of some sort. It was used by the Celts, Romans and Saxons. The Romans used it as a sacrificial altar to their god, Mithras. In recent times it has been used in occult rituals by local covens. Animal bones have been discovered nearby.

Judy Axford and her son, Darren, then seven, suffered an unnerving experience there one hot summer afternoon in 1981. They were with a friend and his son. As the four approached the stones in the hot sun, the temperature suddenly dropped and they felt very cold. Worse than this, a horrible stench of rotting flesh hit them. The smell was so overwhelming that they turned and walked away, young Darren instinctively making the sign of the cross.

ALSO NEARBY - THE HAUNTED HOME OF ALFRED, LORD TENNYSON

Farrington House at Freshwater was once the home of the nineteenth-century Poet Laureate, Alfred, Lord Tennyson. The house established itself in folklore as being the destination for a ghostly horse and carriage. Ron Legg, landlord of the haunted Red Lion pub for many years, was as sceptical as most people – until his experience one frosty moonlit night in 1946.

Cycling along Victoria Road, he heard the sound of horses' hooves coming in his direction. He got off his bike and positioned it across the road, thinking that a horse had escaped from a nearby paddock. The sound grew louder, but no matter how much he strained his eyes he could see nothing. He stood dumbfounded as the sound passed him by. The sound of the hoofbeats changed, as if the horse had left the road and was now on gravel.

Annual Festival

In Newchurch, farm work used to resume after the Twelve Days of Christmas on Plough Monday. Nowadays, on Plough Sunday, the plough is blessed at a special church service.

How to Find Gatcombe

Travel south from Newport on the A3020, and about two miles after the road forks look out for signs for Gatcombe on your right. The church is just past the old Whitecroft Hospital.

Consult Ordnance Survey map 196.

NEAREST MAIN TOURIST INFORMATION CENTRE
The Car Park, Church Litten, Newport, PO30 1JU.
Tel: 01983 525450.

OTHER SITES OF MYSTERIOUS DISAPPEARANCES AND APPEARANCES

On Friday 6 June 1980, miner Zigmund Jan Adamski walked out of his house near Wakefield and disappeared off the face of the earth. He was on an errand to buy some potatoes from a corner shop. Five days later PC Allan Godfrey received a call to attend a coalyard next to Todmorden Railway Station. There the officer discovered the body of a man on top of a fifteen foot high heap of coal. It was Adamski.

According to workers in the yard, the body had appeared sometime in the early afternoon. No one had seen it arrive despite the fact it was daylight and the yard was overlooked by houses. Adamski had inexplicable burn marks on his body, and the inquest concluded an Open Verdict.

There had been a number of UFO sightings over Todmorden at the time, which some people have linked with the death, and curiously, Alan Godfrey himself suffered a UFO abduction experience five months later (see pages 46-7).

The village of Woolpit near Bury St Edmunds in Suffolk has a strange tale associated with it. In the twelfth century, two green children apparently appeared in the village from a hole in the ground. They spoke a language no one could understand, and had difficulty adapting to the local diet. The boy wasted away and died, but the girl survived and learnt English. She told the villagers that she came from a land where all the people were green. There was no sun or moon, just perpetual twilight.

Scotland

THE LOCH NESS BEASTIE

A DEEP, DARK BODY OF WATER

BELIEVER OR SCEPTIC, none can deny that the Loch Ness Monster, affectionately known as Nessie, has become a major British institution. Despite sightings of lake monsters in many other countries, including the USA, Canada, Japan, Sweden and Russia, Nessie is the beast on everyone's lips.

I shall never forget my first visit to Loch Ness. It was a wet July day when I arrived at Fort Augustus, situated at the head of the loch. After parking I walked along a footpath to the water's edge. It was the realization of a boyhood dream. Before me was a body of water 23 miles long, a mile wide and an average depth twice that of the North Sea – stained black with peat particles.

I remember seeing a satirical newspaper cartoon of a coiled serpent with a horse's head when I was a child. I asked my father what it meant, and he told me it referred to a 'monster' that someone had seen in a Scottish lake. I was amazed that my father should comment on the matter without humour, when patently such a thing was absurd.

Over the years the idea of a prehistoric animal surviving into the twentieth century in the depths of a freshwater lake captured my imagination. Now here I stood looking down the loch, crowded in with steep hills that slope a thousand feet on either side. Above hung purple-black storm clouds, while below me eight-foot-high waves crashed on the gravel just yards away. I stayed there for about an hour, hoping for a glimpse of the loch's elusive (or illusive) inhabitant, but finally walked back into the village to find lodgings.

MONSTER HUNTER EXTRAORDINAIRE

A few days later I was driving along the south-eastern shore and saw a sign at Lower Foyers which said: 'LOCH NESS INVESTIGATION – FRANK SEARLE'. There was an arrow pointing down a track which I followed. I had read an article in the *Sunday Times* colour supplement which featured Searle – an ex-army paratrooper turned monster hunter.

The man was instantly likeable and we struck up a friendship which lasted for several years until his mysterious disappearance while treasure hunting in 1985. Frank had left the loch in 1984 after spending fifteen years there entertaining thousands of tourists. Searle spoke with knowledge, humour and enthusiasm about the possibility of several small families of 'Nessies' living in different parts of the loch. Unfortunately he blotted his copybook with several dubious photographs. Frank fell victim to the pressures of monster hunting, where competition between factions is fierce. He called it a 'circus', and he was not the only one to stumble in the ring.

SIGHTINGS OF THE BEASTIE

During subsequent visits to Loch Ness I talked to many of the personalities involved in its investigation. Among them was Betty Gallagher, curator of the Loch Ness Monster Exhibition at Drumnadrochit. She spoke of how easy it is to misinterpret common things as something unusual:

Visitors see monsters left, right and centre. But they're not used to the tricks of the environment. The eye is easily deceived. Normally we receive three or five sightings a year which we consider are probably genuine. When a report is made by one of the locals, used to the environment, we think, 'This is it!' They know what floating logs and freak waves can do to the eye.

Greengrocer and fisherman Jimmy Cameron told me about one of his sightings, which occurred in 1981:

I was driving my van heading towards Loch End in the afternoon. As I came level with a lay-by, the trees were short and leafless, and this gave me a clear view out over the loch. About 600 yards away, I saw clearly a neck and head sticking out of the water about three feet. It was dark brown or black, and the head was flat. I stopped the van at the next lay-by but it had gone. It had been facing towards Dores.

Father Gregory Brusy is Father Prior of the Benedictine Abbey at Fort Augustus. In October 1973 the organist of Westminster Cathedral was staying with him, and one morning they decided to go for a short walk. Father Brusy told me what happened while they were standing on the stone jetty near the abbey, looking out over the bay: 'The water was calm and there was not a boat in sight. Suddenly, about three hundred yards off shore, there was a great churning of the water, then a five-foot length of neck appeared with spray flying everywhere. We observed it for twenty seconds as it began to move away before diving back beneath the water in a sort of curious sideways motion.'

THE SEARCH FOR EVIDENCE

Speculations range from a plesiosaur-type creature, an unusual species of fish, hallucinations caused by electromagnetic energy released by geological faults, and a paranormal explanation. Certainly it involves something more than misidentifications and hoaxes.

Naturalist Adrian Shine has spent many years leading monster-hunting expeditions at Loch Ness and Loch Morar. He gave me his

thoughts on the subject: 'I don't know anything about the paranormal. I'm a naturalist. Possibly we're talking about a large fish.
There is something in the loch of zoological interest – we've
known that for years. We've also known that the alleged evidence
is faulty.' Shine thinks that the 'creature' captured on film by P. A.
Macnab in 1955 (see photograph 12 opposite page 185) could be
an Atlantic Sturgeon – a fish capable of growing up to 20 feet
long.

Some of that faulty 'evidence' Shine mentions includes underwater photographs taken in Urquhart Bay by Dr Robert Rines in
1972 and 1975. These appeared to show a diamond-shaped flipper,
a 'gargoyle-shaped head' and 'upper torso, neck and head' of the
'monster'. What was not generally understood at the time was that
these shots had been 'cleaned up' by computer image enhance-
ment techniques. The 1975 pictures were taken at a location
where a plastic monster sank during the making of *The Private Lives
of Sherlock Holmes*, and where a rotting tree stump was more
recently recovered. This bore a resemblance to Rines' 'gargoyle
head'.

I also talked to Nicholas Witchell, BBC newsreader and Loch
Ness researcher for many years. He originally applauded the
underwater pictures, but then revised his ideas. He said: 'They
should no longer be considered as valid evidence. I now have no
views on what might be in Loch Ness. I just see myself as a journalist recording the experiences and opinions of others.'

One of the most ambitious projects to probe the loch's murky
depths, called Operation Deepscan, was carried out in 1987. Two
parallel rows of boats, fitted with short-operation echo-sounders,
were strung out over the water. Adrian Shine, project leader of the
sonar sweep, reported some interesting soundings. One was a very
strong echo which was not there when the second row of boats
passed over.

In summer 1992 a new sonar sweep of the loch commenced. At
just after seven o'clock in the evening of 27 July something 'large
and solid-sounding' was tracked by the Norwegian vessel *Simrad*
between Foyers and Invermoriston. It was the largest sonar
reading ever made in Loch Ness.

In August 1992 the first camcorder film of Nessie was made. It
was shot from the slope above Urquhart Castle and seems to show

something black and solid churning up the water. Adrian Shine and Steuart Campbell speculated that it might be a freak wave, but zoologist Peter Meadows thought differently. He told the media: 'I'm amazed by what I've seen. I've never seen anything like it before!'

In early 1994, two Loch Ness researchers, David Martin and Alastair Boyd, revealed that the 'surgeon's picture' was a hoax. This famous picture of Nessie was allegedly taken by gynaecologist Robert Wilson in April 1934. It supposedly showed the head and long neck of one of the beasts. According to Christian Spurling, a model maker, the object was in fact a converted clockwork submarine purchased from Woolworth's.

ALSO NEARBY - BOLESKINE HOUSE AND THE BURIAL GROUND

On the south-eastern bank of the loch between Foyers and Inverfarigaig lies Boleskine House, which is visible from the road. The house once belonged to the black magician Aleister Crowley, condemned as the Great Beast 666 foretold in the Book of Revelation.

Crowley, who died in 1947, celebrated the Black Mass and indulged in obscene rituals in this house. He created around him a world of lust, alcoholism, drug addiction, insanity and death. The media dubbed him 'the wickedest man in the world'.

DARK FORCES

Crowley was perhaps the most famous person associated with black magic, but there are hundreds more following in the tradition. These people have a lust for power and seek to experience and control supernatural forces.

Chaos magic is the latest permutation. Adherents practice no safeguards but lay open their minds, throwing themselves into the void. They risk their own sanity in the search for the ultimate experience with occult forces.

Some suggest that the Loch Ness Monster was brought into being by the use of black magic.

8. Highgate Cemetery is one of the most atmospheric places in London. Is it surprising then that rumours of a vampire emerged in the 1970s? (See pages 126–130.)

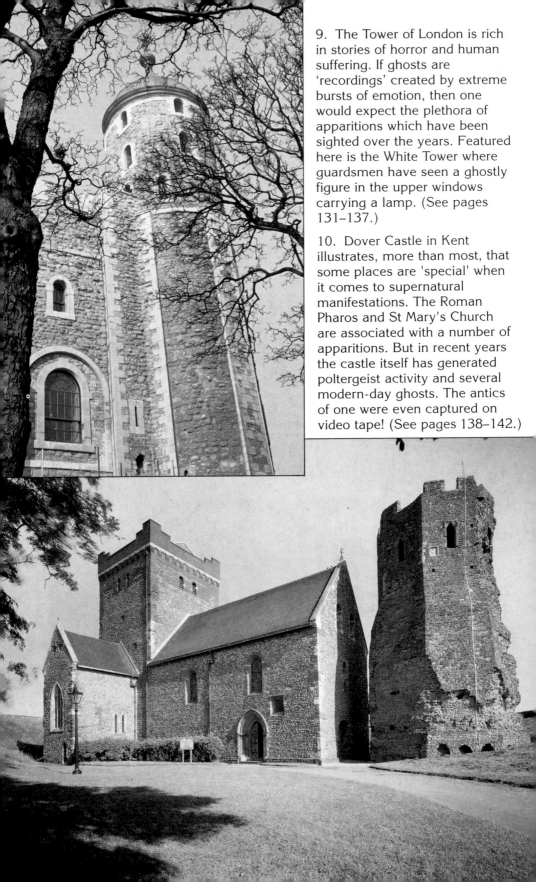

9. The Tower of London is rich in stories of horror and human suffering. If ghosts are 'recordings' created by extreme bursts of emotion, then one would expect the plethora of apparitions which have been sighted over the years. Featured here is the White Tower where guardsmen have seen a ghostly figure in the upper windows carrying a lamp. (See pages 131–137.)

10. Dover Castle in Kent illustrates, more than most, that some places are 'special' when it comes to supernatural manifestations. The Roman Pharos and St Mary's Church are associated with a number of apparitions. But in recent years the castle itself has generated poltergeist activity and several modern-day ghosts. The antics of one were even captured on video tape! (See pages 138–142.)

Boleskine burial ground is on the opposite side of the road, over-looking the loch. The ancient tombstones record the resting places of clan members. It is a strange, eerie place, an ideal location for a horror film. Today it is reputed to be the haunt of witches, and, being so close to Boleskine House, perhaps that is not surprising.

How to Find Loch Ness

Loch Ness is the largest of a string of lakes along a rift in the Earth's crust called the Great Glen. It can be reached on the A82 from Glasgow. This road follows the west coast of Loch Lomond and goes through some of the most beautiful scenery in the British Isles. Look out for the breathtaking sight of Black Mountain on your left. Eventually the road comes to the Great Glen, where you should continue eastwards following the signs to Loch Ness.

From Aberdeen on the east coast, join the A96 which goes directly to Inverness, the capital of the Highlands. Inverness is on the River Ness and from there you can take either the A82 to the northern bank of the loch, or the quieter B852 to Dores on the southern bank.

Consult Ordnance Survey maps 26, 34 and 35.

NEAREST MAIN TOURIST INFORMATION CENTRE
Castle Wynd, Inverness, Highlands. *Tel: 01463 234353.*

OTHER SCOTTISH LAKE MONSTERS

Loch Ness and Loch Morar are not the only places in Scotland reputed to possess lake monsters. In September 1893 Dr Farquhar Matheson and his wife were boating on Loch Alsh in the Grampian region when they saw a giraffe-like head and neck moving through the water. The creature was brown and they noticed a ruffle just behind the head.

According to Scottish folklore a monster lives in Loch Awe off the B840 in Strathclyde. During bad winters when the loch froze over, the sound of cracking ice was believed to be the beast trying to get out.

THE SEARCH FOR MORAG

CRYSTAL CLEAR WATERS

SO MUCH ATTENTION is paid to Loch Ness that little is said or written about Loch Morar. It too has its 'monster', a beast that has been named Morag. One reason for this dearth of interest is the relative inaccessibility of Morar. There are no roads on either shore, except for a track on the north side which peters out after about two miles.

The loch is 11 miles long and has a depth of 1,017 feet, making it the deepest lake in Britain. Unlike Loch Ness its waters are not blackened with peat dye, but crystal-clear. It is a place of beauty and silence, surrounded by gentle mountains that rise to a towering cleft at the loch's head. The Silver Sands of Morar have been immortalized in film and song.

THE LOCH MORAR SURVEY

In 1970 a number of researchers from London University teamed up to conduct the Loch Morar Survey. While the biologists among them carried out a study of the loch's ecology, the rest of the team kept watch from various camera sites and interviewed witnesses. Although there were two brief sightings of 'something', no photographs were produced. However, investigators did collate thirty-three eye-witness reports dating from 1887 through to 1971. The biologists discovered that the loch was not a sterile body of water, but teeming with life – ample food for a family of large predators.

ALTERCATION ON THE LOCH

The sighting which inspired the investigation involved two long-distance lorry drivers. On 16 August 1969, a hot, still day, Duncan MacDonnell and William Simpson had been fishing on Loch Morar. They anticipated no problems returning to their moorings. MacDonnell was steering the motor cruiser while Simpson boiled a kettle of water for tea. Duncan MacDonnell explained to researcher Elizabeth Campbell what happened next:

> I heard a splashing or disturbance in the water astern of us. I looked up and about 20 yards behind us this creature was coming directly after us in our wake. It only took it a matter of seconds to catch up on us. It grazed the side of the boat – I am quite certain this was unintentional. When it struck the boat it seemed to come to a halt or at least slow down. I grabbed the oar and was attempting to fend it off, my one fear being that if it got under the boat it might capsize it.

This was the start of a terrifying experience. The collision had upset the kettle and extinguished the flames. After turning off the gas Simpson rushed on deck to see what the trouble was. He was confronted with the unbelievable sight of his friend trying to fend off the legendary water beast – a creature that belonged to old wives' tales and nightmares, not to reality.

Afterwards the men provided a full description. It was 25–30 feet long, with three humps projecting 18 inches above the water. The creature was covered in rough, dirty brown skin and had a snake-like head about a foot wide at the top.

When MacDonnell's oar snapped, Bill Simpson panicked and grabbed his shotgun. He discharged the barrel at the creature and watched it disappear below the surface of the water. The men only told close relatives of their frightening ordeal, but one of them notified the press and the story received national publicity.

MONSTER EXPLANATIONS

There are three categories of explanation for lake monster sightings; psychological, physical, and paraphysical.

- Psychological: witnesses are tricked by unusual conditions in the environment. Researcher Anne Arnold Silk added a new twist to this idea. Faults in the earth's crust run right across the Highlands and she speculates that standing wave formations created by seismic stress could create the illusion of something large moving in the water.

- Physical: the beasts are actual marine animals which have survived from prehistoric times, similar to the plesiosaur or a large unknown species of fish.

- Paraphysical: lake monsters are temporary psychic constructions created by the collective unconscious.

See also *Loch Ness*, page 164 and *Bala*, page 194.

SIGHTINGS AND DOWSING

The Loch Morar Survey team returned for their third summer in 1972. It was during this expedition that Elizabeth Campbell had her own sighting, on 19 July.

Again it was a hot, sunny day with calm conditions. Ms Campbell was manning a camera set up on a headland beside White Beach. To the east was a small bay known locally as Caravan Bay. Over to the west two boats belonging to the team were carrying out sonar experiments. At seven minutes past ten she became aware of a long, thin, black object near some rocks off Caravan Bay. Investigator Tim Dinsdale reported her story: 'The object was stationary for such a long time that I began to wonder if it was the top of some more rocks that I hadn't previously noticed. I also noticed a long white streak tailing back from the object – the sort of streak you sometimes get after a power boat has gone by. The object itself was only a few inches above the water, and about six to seven feet long.'

She could not take any photographs because she would have

been shooting directly into the sun. Two minutes later the object had vanished. A breeze had stirred up, and she wondered if it had caused a swell to hide the unusual 'rocks'.

And then, about ten minutes later, I saw what looked like the same long thin black object, only this time farther away. Looking through binoculars I saw that it was beginning to move; it was now a definite low-lying hump, about six feet across and not more than 18 inches high, moving diagonally round the headland at about one or two knots. Although it went so slowly there was a distinct low, white wash.

Some researchers doubt that physical prehistoric animals exist in any of the lakes where sightings have been recorded. They believe that the phenomenon is paraphysical. The body of water is at the centre of an energy field that responds to thought and in response conjures up temporary mythical beasties. These 'monsters' are not holograms, but possess mass, and are able to interact with the environment. They exist for seconds, or minutes at the most.

Ron Halliday, then a member of the Scottish group Strange Phenomena Investigations, went dowsing at Loch Morar with other members during June and July 1990. Dowsers believe they can tune into invisible lines of energy. Most carry rods which amplify any response like a needle on a dial. Dowsers have been successful in detecting underground streams and minerals, and Ron claims to have discovered a buried prehistoric standing stone.

At Loch Morar the SPI team received responses which, according to Ron, 'took my breath away, almost literally at times'. He continued: 'All around the loch side, north and south, the indications from movement of the dowsing rods were that regularly spaced lines of unknown energy passed from the hill sides into the loch, and, I suspect, travelled across (or under) Loch Morar to emerge on the opposite bank.'

Despite the dearth of potential witnesses, the sightings continue. In August 1990, for five minutes Duncan McKellaig and three other people observed an unknown object in the loch 50–100 yards away.

How to Find Loch Morar

Loch Morar is on the west coast of Scotland and, like Loch Ness, was once open to the sea. From Glasgow take the A82 to Fort William, which will take you through some of the most beautiful scenery in Scotland. From there follow the A830 past Loch Eil and Loch Eilt for about 30 miles. Morar is located just a few miles before the road ends at Mallaig on the coast. There are a number of guest houses and a youth hostel at Morar.

Consult Ordnance Survey map 40.

Annual Events and Festivals

1 August: Mallaig and Morar Highland Games by Loch Morar.

NEAREST MAIN TOURIST INFORMATION CENTRE
Cameron Centre, Cameron Square, Fort William, Highlands.
Tel: 01397 703781.

MORE SCOTTISH LAKE MONSTERS

Loch Borralan, south east of Ledmore, is accessed by the A837. This is the place where fishermen fell prey to a water horse. One story tells of two fishermen who saw the horse and were entranced by its beauty. They disappeared that day leaving their tackle and a tell-tale hoofprint behind.

According to legend, the water horse of Loch Garve, near Strathpeffer in the Highlands, carried off a beautiful girl. There she lived beneath the surface in a house belonging to the horse. When she complained it was too cold, her captor brought down a mason who built a fireplace and chimney! That, so the story goes, explains why the water at the eastern end of the Loch never freezes.

Two miles from the famous ski resort of Aviemore lies Loch Pityoulish which also has its own water horse tale. The water horse enticed people into the loch while masquerading as a real horse. One victim is said to have escaped by cutting off the fingers of his hand which would not let go of the beast's reins.

THE DARK SECRET OF GLAMIS CASTLE

A MURDERED KING

THE TAPESTRY of mystery and horror that is woven into the fabric of Glamis Castle reads like something from a Gothic novel. The castle itself is an awesome sight, set in the wooded vale of Strathmore on Tayside, against a background of the Grampian Mountains. As you approach along the tree-lined drive its battlements and towers soar up before your eyes. It is a fairytale castle, a dark, brooding place, reputedly one of the most haunted houses in the land (see photograph 13 opposite page 185).

Glamis is also Scotland's oldest inhabited castle, and has for centuries been the ancestral home of the Bowes-Lyon family, Earls of Strathmore. More recently, Princess Margaret was born there – the Queen Mother was born a Bowes-Lyon. The castle's reputation of horror goes back to 1034, when King Malcolm II was assassinated by a group of disloyal subjects – cut down with claymores and left bleeding to death. The floorboards in 'King Malcolm's Room' still bear a stain of blood – although it is unlikely to have been Malcolm's, as the flooring was at some stage replaced. The murder was immortalized in Shakespeare's *Macbeth*.

THE FAMILY CURSE

In 1372, King Robert II gave Glamis to his son-in-law, Sir John Lyon, whose family had until then lived at Forteviot. When they moved they took with them a chalice which brought the family luck – as long as it remained in Forteviot. At Glamis it became a curse.

Various incidents were ascribed to the 'poisoned chalice'. Sir John was killed in a duel in 1383. One hundred and fifty years later Janet Douglas – Lady Glamis – was burned at the stake in Edinburgh on the orders of James V, who was convinced she was a witch. It is her spectre, the 'grey lady', which has been seen along the castle corridors.

The 3rd Earl of Strathmore was responsible for encouraging belief in the curse during the late seventeenth century. A notorious gambler, Patrick was playing cards with the Earl of Crawford when a servant reminded him that the Sabbath was approaching. Patrick's reply was that they would play on, and the Devil could join them if he so wished. When midnight came, the Devil appeared and told the Earls that they had forfeited their souls, and that after their deaths they would play cards until Judgement Day.

Rumour persists of a secret room where the gambling took place. In 1957 Florence Foster, a servant at the castle, told a news-

CURSES

It has long been a belief that some objects have the ability to give their owners 'bad luck'. For example, in the 1970s portraits of a little boy crying were said to be connected to many house fires in Britain. Firemen noticed the same picture hanging in many burnt-out houses. Media exposure encouraged people to get rid of the 'cursed' prints.

There are also many old houses in Britain that are home to cursed human skulls. The skulls behave themselves as long as they are not removed. When this happens, as it did at Wardley Hall, Cheshire, for instance, calamities befall the inhabitants.

The most famous cursed objects were artifacts removed from the tomb of Tutankhamen. Several archaeologists died mysteriously as a result.

paper that she would stay awake at night hearing the Earls 'rattling dice, stamping and swearing'. Finally she could take it no longer and gave in her notice.

A daughter of Lord Castletown claimed to have seen the ghost of the Earl of Crawford – a huge bearded figure. The elder sister of the Queen Mother described how children would awake screaming in the castle, and talk of an old bearded man leaning over their beds. Sir Shane Bowes-Lyon spoke of the apparition appearing to his Aunt Mary.

CASTLE OF TERROR

Over the years the castle has been the location for many horrors. There is one tale of a grey-bearded man, shackled and left to starve, whose spirit appeared simultaneously to two witnesses at the turn of the century. One of these was Mrs MacLagan, wife of the then Archbishop of York. Other guests, including Queen Elizabeth the Queen Mother, have been disturbed over the years by bumps, raps and footsteps in the dead of night.

In another gruesome tale a party of Ogilvies arrived at the castle and begged protection from the Lindsay clan, to which the inhabitants belonged. Believing him to be an ally, they allowed the Earl to lead them into the castle depths. But they were locked in a chamber and left to die – not before some had turned cannibal and eaten the bodies of their comrades. This dreadful crime remained a secret for a long time until a late Lord Strathmore was led to the sealed room by the sounds of terrifying screams and bangings – the sounds of the tortured spirits. When the unventilated chamber was opened the Earl is said to have collapsed with nausea and shock. Since then it has been known as the Haunted Chamber. Does the apparition of an emaciated figure, nicknamed Jack the Runner, have any connection with this horror?

Other ghosts include a negro pageboy and a 'white lady' who haunts the clock tower, a 'grey lady' who resides in the chapel, and a tall figure in a long black coat who has been seen disappearing through a locked door. But more than the hauntings, more even than the murders and cruelty, Glamis Castle is notorious for one all-pervading dark secret: the family 'monster'.

A MONSTROUS SECRET

Such is the shame of this secret that no recent Earl has spoken of it to outsiders. The nature of the horror is only passed on to a Strathmore heir on his twenty-first birthday, and no female member of the family has been told the secret.

In less enlightened times physical deformity was seen as a reflection of evil – the result of a curse, or punishment by God for some wrongdoing. Either way, it was a source of embarrassment and shame; such an affliction was best driven from thought and hidden from sight.

Rumours abounded in the nineteenth century that Patrick had to cope with another horror before his tussle with the Devil. They said he had fathered a deformed child, which had been locked away from prying eyes and lived to a great age. If the rumours are true, it is a dark secret that Patrick flirted with. Evidence for this relies on the interpretation of a painting in the drawing room of Glamis Castle. The picture features the 3rd Earl, seated, wearing a bronze breastplate. Standing to his right is the figure of a tall man. He too wears a breastplate, but it seems to fit a torso which is deformed. This impression is reinforced by a right arm which looks foreshortened.

Claude Bowes-Lyon, the 13th Earl, was obsessed by the family horror. He paid a workman and his family to emigrate to Australia, after the man had come across a hidden room behind the chapel whose contents filled him with terror. Claude told a friend who was being inquisitive: 'If you could guess the nature of the secret, you would go down on your knees and thank God it were not yours.'

It was Claude who broke with tradition and told his estate manager, Gavin Ralston, details of the scandal. The man was so appalled that afterwards he refused to stay overnight in the castle. Ralston told the 14th Earl's daughter-in-law: 'It is lucky that you do not know and can never know it, for if you did you would not be a happy woman.'

Perhaps the truth concerned not one deformed child, but two or more. Maybe the horror was that a genetic mutation plagued the Bowes-Lyon line.

How to Find Glamis Castle

Glamis is about one and a half hours' drive from Edinburgh. Take the A90, then the M90 to Perth. At Perth get on to the M85 and then join the A93 going north. About two miles later turn right on to the A94, leading straight into Glamis village, which houses the Angus Folk Museum. The castle is open every day between 1 April and 30 October from 10.30 a.m.

Consult Ordnance Survey map 54.

NEAREST MAIN TOURIST INFORMATION CENTRE
4 City Square, Dundee. *Tel: 01382 27723.*

OTHER HAUNTED SCOTTISH CASTLES

There are other reputedly haunted castles in Scotland. Craigievar Castle at Lumphanan, Grampian, was built by the Forbes in the seventeenth century, and is now owned by the National Trust.

The Blue Room is haunted by a member of the Gordon family – traditional enemies of the Forbes. He was forced through a window by the third laird, Red Sir John, to fall four stories to his death. In 1982, Lady Cecilia Sempill, last of the family to live in the castle, related a personal experience.

The family were in financial trouble and Lady Sempill was talking matters over with their solicitor in the drawing room one evening. Opposite the hall door she saw a man in a kilt. She called out thinking it was Lord Sempill, but the figure walked off. When she followed him into the poorly lit hallway it was full of people dressed in unfamiliar clothes. Lady Cecilia pushed through the throng still looking for her 'husband'. Suddenly she felt exhausted and returned to her bemused guest. After offering the solicitor a drink, she went up to bed where she found Lord Sempill fast asleep. She later learned it was a tradition that her ancestors would return to the castle if the family came into difficulty.

Other castles with supernatural reputations include Fyvie Castle, Brodie Castle and Crathes Castle, Grampian; Culzean Castle, Ayrshire; Brodick Castle, Isle of Arran and Inveraray Castle, Strathclyde.

THE BONNYBRIDGE UFO INVASION

A SECOND WARMINSTER

*I*N *1992* the Scottish town of Bonnybridge became the centre of attention, with a wave of UFO sightings which are still occurring. Since then, newspaper, radio and television reporters have visited the area recording eyewitness accounts. Many of the sightings have been collated by Councillor Billy Buchanan, and investigated by paranormal researcher Malcolm Robinson, who told me he believes something strange is definitely going on. He described Bonnybridge as another Warminster, a place where UFOs were seen during the sixties and seventies (see pages 102-109).

CATALOGUE OF SIGHTINGS

What follows is a selection of sightings throughout the area. Although most of them date from 1992, there were several prominent cases before that year. The first one narrated here dates from 1989.

1989: The case involved a fire crew attending a blaze on Gardrum Moss near the village of Shieldhill. According to one fire officer, he and fifteen of his colleagues at first saw a small red

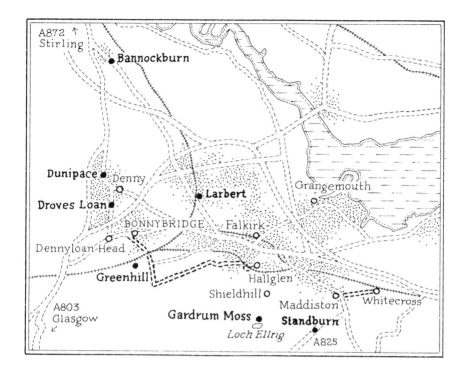

object hovering in the distance. It then began moving towards the fire engine, gathering speed, before turning west.

A second, white object appeared, heading towards nearby Loch Ellrig. It hovered about six feet above the water, just 20 feet from the fire crew. Suddenly the object rushed towards them, making a ninety-degree turn at the last moment.

Shaken by the experience, as the crew were about to leave they noticed a third object, also white, which flew directly overhead in a 'jerky movement'. Interviewed by Malcolm Robinson, the officer said that the crew received the strong impression that the objects were under intelligent control, and were observing their activities.

January 1992: At around 9 p.m. Jim Walker was driving from Dennyloan Head to Denny. About halfway he approached a junction called Droves Loan. Hovering above it was a 'bright cluster of lights'. He assumed it was a helicopter and passed right under it. Further down the road he pulled over and climbed out for a better look. The object was silent, very low and spanned the full width of the road. The light display was in the form of a pyramid.

March 1992: Three members of the Sloggett family – mother, daughter and son – had two encounters on a back road from Hallglen to Bonnybridge.

In the first incident, Steven Sloggett noticed a large circle of light in the sky at about 7 p.m. He pointed it out to his mother and sister, and they watched as it landed nearby. Curiously they did not investigate, and continued walking towards Bonnybridge. Looking back, they saw a large blue light 'sitting on the road'. It was very intense and about the size of a basketball. A wire fence close to the phenomenon began rattling. The family also heard other strange sounds, including a whirring, a noise similar to a door opening, and then a howl. At this point they took to their heels!

Later that month the Sloggetts were on the same road again, but half a mile nearer to Bonnybridge. Suddenly an 'object' came out of some trees and flashed a light at them. The daughter, Carole, told reporters: 'We heard a whirring and chains rattling. This big truck thing, like a huge Tonka toy, came out of the trees and something flashed, as if we'd been photographed.'

20 September 1992: Steven Wilson, accompanied by his friend David Gillespie, was driving from Whitecross to Maddiston when they noticed a peculiar red object hovering over a field near a housing estate. It was oval and sharply defined. The men heard no sound and observed it for about one and a half minutes.

27 October 1992: Patrick Forsyth and his two young sons were driving to Stirling on the A872. They had just left Dunipace when an object appeared 100 yards in front of their car, 25 – 40 feet above the road. It was black, circular and two-tiered, with a row of green lights around it. Suddenly a fog bank appeared in front of the car. Patrick watched as the vehicle in front went into the bank and skidded to one side. As they followed it, one of the boys watched the object receding very quickly in the direction of Grangemouth.

11 November 1992: James Thomson was in the Greenhill area of Bonnybridge that evening when he observed two huge bright lights coming towards him. They were roughly 200 feet high as they passed over a nearby field, moving from side to side. James saw some smaller lights on top of the object, and heard a hum similar to the noise that a washing machine makes on its final spin.

CLOSE ENCOUNTERS

Professor Allen Hynek of the Centre for UFO Studies (CUFOS) devised the UFO classification system used by Steven Spielberg for his film:

- Close Encounters of the First Kind – the UFO is seen at close range but there is no interaction with the environment.

- Close Encounters of the Second Kind – here the object damages the environment, burns observers or interferes with mechanical or electrical equipment such as motor vehicles.

- Close Encounters of the Third Kind – beings are observed in or near the object.

- Close Encounters of the Fourth Kind – a later addition to Hynek's system. A 'CE4' is where an observer is apparently abducted by UFO entities.

15 November 1992: At 6 p.m. in Standburn, near Falkirk, Mr Napier and his daughter observed an oval object with three red lights set in a triangular configuration at the front, and flashing white lights at the rear. It was at first quite high in the sky before moving towards the ground. They watched it for ten minutes and heard a humming sound. Then it flew off at a fast rate across a field on the opposite side of the road.

17 January 1993: In Bannockburn, a few miles north of Bonnybridge, a family watched in awe as a UFO hovered over their home. Nine-year-old David Young was outside playing in the snow. At about 9.15 p.m. his mother, Mary, went out to call him in. Mary explained: 'I shouted to David and he turned to me and said, "Mum, look at that car in the sky!" I looked up and saw bright lights, just like car lights, about 40 feet above the houses.'

She called her boyfriend, Kevin, who came outside with her daughter, Jacqueline. Kevin speculated that it might be an aircraft, but quickly realized that could not be the case. Mary described it as oval with a square of red lights underneath. Inside this was a square of white lights. There were also two white lights at the front and two at the rear of the object. Five minutes later it sped off, making a humming sound.

BONNYBRIDGE UFO ON VIDEO

At last someone managed to film one of the objects. Just after 7 p.m. on 19 January 1994, twenty-seven-year-old Jim Rogers started the short drive to his father's house in Larbert. His attention was suddenly drawn to a very bright white object which seemed to be pacing his car. As he approached a junction the interior of the vehicle was suddenly lit up by a powerful light. Jim put his foot down and raced the rest of the way.

As soon as he arrived he ran into the house and shouted for everyone to come outside. They watched as the object came towards the house, making a humming sound. At this point Jim's sister appeared with a video camera, joined by Linda, his wife, with her camera. There were six witnesses altogether, and all of them were certain it was not a conventional aircraft.

Malcolm Robinson has examined Linda's film, the best of the two, which lasts about 18 seconds. It shows initially a white light, which appears to eject a smaller light. Then Linda zooms into the object and what appears is a vertical cylindrical object, lit in the middle. Just as it disappears, the object seems to dip and turn.

WAS IT A BIRD? WAS IT A PLANE?

Inevitably there is speculation that some of the more innocuous sightings can be accounted for by military aircraft. Certainly that is probably the case in some instances. But many of the sightings depict an object that makes little noise and has the ability to hover, and suddenly change direction. No known aircraft fits that pattern.

In recent years there has been speculation about a top-secret American aircraft codenamed Aurora. It has supposedly been flown from a base in Scotland, but the authorities deny that the aircraft even exists. According to rumour, Aurora possesses the manoeuvrability that could account for the Bonnybridge UFOs. The obvious question is: why should a top-secret aircraft be lit up, making its presence obvious?

11. The Long Man of Wilmington, East Sussex, dates back to antiquity, and seems to be part of a magical landscape once manipulated by medieval monks. Today pilgrims visit Wilmington to try to lock into its power. (See pages 143–149.)

12. Glamis Castle in Tayside, Scotland, has a dark history shrouded in horror and mystery. It is the place where Macbeth allegedly murdered Duncan and where an Earl played cards with the Devil. There is a monstrous family secret and a rich variety of ghosts borne out of torture and violent death. (See pages 175–179.)

13. One of the few Loch Ness monster photographs that so far has stood the test of time! Bank Manager and Ayrshire County Councillor Mr P. A. Macnab took two photographs in the early afternoon of Friday, 29 July 1955. The loch was flat calm when he noticed something swimming on the surface, heading towards Urquhart Castle. He received so much ridicule that he destroyed the second picture. (See pages 164–169.)

ALSO NEARBY – STIRLING CASTLE

Haunted Stirling Castle is approximately 10 miles north of Bonnybridge up the M80. Mary Queen of Scots was crowned there in 1543. A woman in a pink dress has been seen walking from the castle to the church, and a 'green lady' haunts other parts of the castle. Her appearance seems to precede disasters, such as fires, in the castle. People have also heard unaccountable footsteps, and in 1820 a sentry was discovered dead with a look of terror on his face.

How to Find Bonnybridge

Bonnybridge itself is just outside Falkirk. If you are coming from Glasgow take the A80, then at the junction with the M80 turn right on to the A803 for three miles to Bonnybridge. If coming from Edinburgh, take the M9 and come off at Junction 5. Turn right on to the A803 and go through Falkirk to Bonnybridge. The sightings have all occurred in and around Bonnybridge.

See map on page 181 and also consult Ordnance Survey map 65.

NEAREST MAIN TOURIST INFORMATION CENTRE
The Steeple, High Street, Falkirk, West Lothian. *Tel: 01324 620244.*
41 Dumbarton Road, Stirling. *Tel: 01786 475019.*

OTHER UFO SIGHTINGS IN SCOTLAND

Colin Wright and Garry Woods were motoring on the A70 between Balerno and Tarbrax near Edinburgh on the night of 17 August 1992. As they rounded a blind bend they were alarmed to see a thirty foot saucer twenty feet above the road. When their car entered a 'shimmering silver curtain' beneath the object, they were enveloped by total blackness. A cassette playing in the car reduced in volume and the vehicle shuddered until they came out the other side. Colin Wright told Scottish investigator Malcolm Robinson that while they were inside the curtain, his seat belt had become unbuckled. This event has all of the hallmarks of a UFO abduction experience.

Muchalls is a small village on the north-east coast ten miles south of Aberdeen. Tom Allen, a senior lecturer and engineer, had his first sighting on the night of 13 December 1971. He was walking to his house on the outskirts of the village when he saw several strange red lights either side of the road. One swooped down from above Burn of Pheppie Farm. A further shock awaited Tom when he was confronted by a tall glowing figure which melted before him.

Tom's sister returned with him, and she too saw the lights. One of them was recognisable as an object the size of a car. In 1975 Tom moved away from the area to go to college, but when he returned to Muchalls during holidays he observed the lights again. Several other villagers have come forward with UFO sightings from around the same time.

THE HORROR IN DECHMONT WOODS

WOODLAND'S DARK SECRET

IN 1979 SOMETHING so strange, so frightening, happened in Dechmont Law Park that it put the town of Livingston on the map. That something involved a UFO, a physical assault, marks left on the ground, a police investigation and forensic analysis of clothing and soil samples. The story has been filmed for *Arthur C. Clarke's Mysterious World* and the LWT television series *Strange But True?* It was the first incident of its kind to be commemorated with a plaque.

Livingston, a small but expanding town just six miles west of Edinburgh off the M8, is a centre for the electronics and high technology industry. To an extent it is a manufactured town, spaciously laid out and surrounded by managed woodland. It was in trees north of the town, close to the M8, that the supernatural intruded on the morning of Friday, 9 November.

Just south of the site is Dechmont Law itself – a hill over 600 feet high which was originally a volcanic plug. This is the highest point in Livingston, and from its summit on a clear day the Lomond Hills in Fife and the Forth Bridges can be seen.

The park is full of wildlife, and in spring, wild flowers such as wood sorrel and pink purslane carpet the woodland floor. It is just

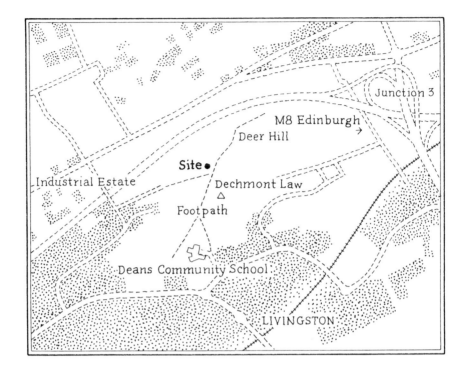

the sort of place in ages past that might hide a wicked witch's cottage. In this twentieth-century fairy story, the cottage was a domed UFO and its occupants much stranger, although just as sinister as anything the Brothers Grimm might have written.

INTRUSION FROM ANOTHER PLACE

Once upon a time there was a poor woodcutter . . .

Sixty-one-year-old Bob Taylor worked for the forestry department of the Livingston Development Corporation, and his job included patrolling Dechmont Law Park to look for stray animals. That morning he drove his van to the edge of the wood and set out on foot, accompanied by his dog.

But as he turned into a clearing he was suddenly overwhelmed with the unexpected. There, on the ground, sat a dull grey, metallic, dome-shaped object. It was about 20 feet wide, with a rim near the base from which projected several antennae or propellers.

A silence descended over the clearing. There was not a sign of life from the object. This, perhaps, made it even harder to bear. Bob stood staring dumbstruck at the machine, and as he did so, incredibly, parts of it began to fade in and out, so that he caught fleeting glimpses of the trees behind it.

As he turned to leave, two spherical objects appeared from the UFO. About a foot in diameter, they were covered in sharp spikes similar in appearance to a sea mine. As they rolled towards him he could hear a sucking sound as the spikes stuck in the wet earth. Before he could escape they were upon him. Over the next few moments three things happened. He felt a tugging, dragging sensation on his legs, tasted and smelt a foul gas, and then collapsed face-down. Just before passing out, Bob thought he heard a swishing sound.

When he came around, his dog was by his side in an excitable and nervous state. Thankfully the objects had gone. When Bob tried to stand his legs felt like jelly, and he was suffering from a severe thirst and a pounding headache. These are all post-anaesthetic symptoms.

Eventually he reached the van and tried to radio for help. But Bob found he could not speak. Then he started the vehicle and attempted to drive home. This was a mistake. He was so weak and disorientated that the van ended up in a ditch. After crawling out, he managed to stagger the remaining distance home. Mrs Taylor looked in horror at the condition of her husband.

Feeling a little better, he took off his clothes so that he could have a bath. They were covered in mud and his trousers were unaccountably ripped. Mrs Taylor telephoned his boss, Malcolm Drummond, and told him that Bob had been attacked. Mr Drummond called the police.

AN INVESTIGATION INTO CRIMINAL ASSAULT

Within minutes of the call seven police officers, headed by Detective Inspector Ian Wark, were on the case. They talked to Bob Taylor and visited the location. There, ladder-like marks were discovered on the ground with twenty to thirty holes such as might have been made with sharp spikes. The police made sketches of the traces and cordoned off the area. Bob's trousers were sent away for forensic analysis.

A doctor who called to examine Bob referred him to Edinburgh Royal Infirmary. But he left when he discovered they wanted to X-ray his skull for a non-existent head injury. The specialist thought Bob was hallucinating.

Over the weekend the case attracted intense media attention. UFO sceptic Steuart Campbell told interviewers he thought that ball lightning was the explanation, even though it did not fit the facts. On the Tuesday, members of the UFO Investigators' Network (UFOIN), arrived at Livingston and carried out their own enquiries.

It had snowed during Monday. With the help of Bob Taylor and colleagues from the forestry department, Andy Collins, Martin Keatman and local investigator Malcolm Robinson patiently removed the snow to reveal the imprints. They also discovered drag marks where Bob had fallen. It looked as if he had been pulled along the ground head first towards the object, his feet gouging out the earth. The holes were in tandem with the marks. All these were measured and photographed.

The investigators were allowed into the police forensics laboratory in Edinburgh to talk with scientists. They were told that the trousers were police issue and therefore very thick. There was a tear at either hip that corresponded with the scratches on Bob's body. The tears had been made in an upwards direction, as if two spikes caught in the material had dragged the unconscious man, head first, towards the UFO.

AFTERMATH

Bob made a full physical recovery, although both he and the dog were off their food for six days after the incident. What happened while he was unconscious? Hypnotic regression was attempted to explore any possible amnesia, but there was an impenetrable blackness which could not be pierced.

UFO PERCIPIENTS

The results of a study into UFO encounter percipients were published in 1993. The study was carried out by the Psychology Department of Carlton University, Ottowa. It concluded:

- There was no difference between the fantasy lives of percipients and people who had not encountered UFOs.
- UFO percipients were slightly more intelligent than other people.
- Percipients were no more likely to suffer from mental disorders than non-percipients.
- People who reported UFOs were more likely to believe in the paranormal.

See also *Ilkley Moor*, page 40, for another well-known abduction case.

The case received such widespread publicity and respect from official investigators that, at the instigation of Scottish ufologists, a plaque was mounted at the site. Unfortunately it was subsequently stolen, but the Livingston Development Corporation are replacing it.

I have spoken to most of those involved in the case, and none told me they thought it was a hallucination. Hallucinations do not leave marks on the ground.

How to Find Livingston

If travelling from either Edinburgh or Glasgow, take the M8 and come off at Junction 3 or 3a, then follow the signs to Dechmont Law Park. There is a public car park next to Deans Community High School. Take the footpath north at right-angles to the car park. The site is approximately 700 yards further on your left, just past the junction with another path heading west.

See map on page 188 and also consult Ordnance Survey maps 65 and 57.

NEAREST MAIN TOURIST INFORMATION CENTRE
Edinburgh and Scotland Information Centre, 3 Princes Street, Edinburgh. *Tel. 0131 557 1700.*

OTHER UFO CLOSE ENCOUNTER CASES

A 'Close Encounter of the Third Kind' near Winchester in Hampshire was extensively investigated in 1976. It concerned a middle-aged couple, Joyce Bowles and Ted Pratt, who were motoring down Chilcomb Road off the A272 on the evening of Sunday 14 November. Just before nine, the car suddenly began shuddering and shaking, then it careered sideways on to a grass verge.

The engine started to roar uncontrollably and the headlights blazed much brighter than normal. Then they noticed a cigar-shaped object a few yards away. Through some windows three faces looked out at them. A bearded humanoid wearing a silver one-piece suit came out of the object and walked towards the car and stared in at the terrified couple. Then the 'man' and the object were gone, and eventually the couple were able to drive away.

On the night of 27 October 1974 the Avis family, a young married couple with three children, was motoring home after visiting relatives in Harold Hill near London. They were heading towards Aveley in Essex. It was only a twenty-minute drive, but as they neared the village they spotted a pale blue oval light which passed over the lonely road in front of them. Suddenly they entered a bank of green mist. On their arrival home, the family discovered that three hours had disappeared. Under hypnosis an abduction scenario emerged. Apparently, their car had been transported upwards in a column of light inside a large 'craft'. There, the family had been separated and given medical examinations by strange-looking entities. Afterwards they were given a tour of the 'ship', then released in their car with no conscious memory of the event.

Wales

THE MONSTER OF LLYN TEGID

THE DEEPEST LAKE IN WALES

BALA LAKE (Llyn Tegid) is part of the Snowdonia National Park in North Wales. It is popular with fishermen and those interested in more active water sports. The small market town of Bala is an international centre for canoeing, sailing and windsurfing, and is also popular with walkers. There is a new leisure complex catering for all these interests.

About five miles long, a mile wide and 150 feet deep, this freshwater lake is the largest in Wales. The main Dolgellau road runs along its northern shore, where there are large lay-bys for tourists to park. On the southern shore is the Bala Lake Railway.

Although it is a natural lake, there is a legend that its waters hide a palace once occupied by a cruel prince. In recent years people have become convinced that something else lives in its depths. They believe the lake is home to a prehistoric monster.

SIGHTINGS OF 'LLABGOCH'

The first sightings of something strange were towards the end of the 1960s, and then tailed off at the beginning of the 1980s. This in itself is odd, unless the 'creature' was paranormal rather than flesh and blood. Whatever the cause of the phenomena, the reports are convincing. Most of the sightings have been by local people who know the lake well, and are familiar with the tricks that the natural environment can play on perceptions.

Two local fishermen had the fright of their lives out on the lake one day. Edward Hughes and his cousin, Meyrick Lewis, were relaxing in their boat about 200 yards from shore. Suddenly something surfaced close to the boat, and they made for the safety of the shore. They said it was huge and could easily have capsized them. The men were so frightened that they sold the boat and have never ventured out on the lake since.

What was it in the lake that could capsize a boat with two grown men in it? Anne Jones of Wenallt Fawr, Cwm Main, saw 'something beautiful similar to a dolphin' while in the company of her sister-in-law. The description that J. M. Rowlands of Bala gave was somewhat different. He saw the head of a creature rising from the water just 15 yards away: 'It was larger than a man's head and the most striking feature were the large eyes looking straight at me.'

Latin teacher Gareth Wyn Jones, of Ysgol y Berwyn, went to the lake with his wife Jill to paint the landscape. After half an hour they were disturbed by a noise as of a shoal of fish jumping. They looked up and saw a huge creature, the colour of an eel, moving slowly across the lake.

Two humps were visible, about 8 yards apart. Between them the water was bubbling as if the beast required great energy to move. They watched it for about fifteen minutes. When it was just a stone's throw away it sank from sight. Afterwards, Gareth sketched what they had seen.

As the sightings mounted the beast was given a name, 'Llabgoch'. Long before the Bala Lake monster, Welsh parents would scare their children with threats that the Llabgoch – a supernatural monster – would get them if they misbehaved.

A more official witness to the creature was Dewi Bowen, the warden of Bala Lake. He told reporter Eifion Glyn about a group of fishermen who caught some small fish in the lake to use as bait the following day. They left the fish in a keep net overnight. In the morning the fish were gone and the net was ripped to shreds. But Dewi Bowen remembers more vividly his own sighting of the thing in 1977.

He was in his office at the time, talking to the car park attendant.

Suddenly they saw 'something massive' break the surface about 200 yards away. The men were astounded. They jumped into a car and drove along the shore for a closer view. But by the time they arrived, the thing had gone.

LAKE MONSTERS INTERNATIONAL

Lake monsters have been sighted in almost every country including North America, Canada, Japan, Russia and Sweden.

A monster known as Manipogo haunts Lake Manitoba in Canada, and in British Columbia lives his cousin, Ogopogo, seen by many reliable witnesses in Okanagan Lake.

Lake Vorota in eastern Siberia has a monster. Witnesses have described a dark grey body, 32 feet long.

The best-known lake in Sweden for monsters is Storsjo. One of the most memorable encounters resulted in Fisheries Officer, Ragnar Bjorks, hitting the beast with his oar.

The first film of a Japanese monster was taken in January 1991 at Lake Ideka. Two long dark shapes were captured on nine minutes of video film taken by Hideaki Tomiyasu and his family.

MONSTER EXPLANATIONS

Sceptics have come up with the familiar answer that people were seeing two otters swimming, one behind the other. During his many years as Warden Dewi Bowen has only seen one otter on the lake, and never two swimming in this fashion. Others have suggested that seals are the answer. During the First World War these animals were trained at Glanllyn to track down submarines. Could some of them have escaped to Llyn Tegid and successfully bred? This is highly unlikely, as seals give birth on land and they would have been discovered long ago.

Those who argue that the beast is prehistoric point out that the lake is host to a fish found nowhere else – the gwyniad. If that could survive there, why not something larger. But the problem remains: why were sightings only made during a fifteen-year period? Or is Llabgoch a purely marine creature, which only surfaces accidentally? Perhaps the reactions of its human observers persuaded it to remain well beneath the surface. If so, it could appear again – at any time.

How to Find Llyn Tegid

Llyn Tegid – Bala Lake – is on the A494 about 17 miles east of Dolgellau. From Mold, follow the road south-west through Ruthin.

Consult Ordnance Survey map 125.

NEAREST MAIN TOURIST INFORMATION CENTRE
Ruthin Craft Centre, Park Road, Ruthin, Clywd, LL15 1BB.
Tel: 01824 703992.

OTHER WELSH LAKE MONSTERS

Lake monster hunters looking for evidence need go no further than Brynberian. There, according to folklore, lies a water monster's grave! Supposedly the creature was captured near a bridge in the village and taken up the mountain for burial. The prehistoric chambered tomb is a few hundred yards south-east of Brynberian village on moorland.

Lly Cynwch, north of Dolgellau in Ewynedd, once reputedly possessed a water monster. Unfortunately, during one of its forays into the hills, a shepherd beheaded the creature with an axe.

STRANGE LIGHTS AND SEA MONSTERS AT BARMOUTH

RETURN OF THE DRAGON

*B*ARMOUTH, once a busy fishing port, is now a seaside town with a quaint, old-fashioned atmosphere. The coast round about has produced a number of sightings of a sea monster and other strange phenomena.

According to a Welsh book entitled *The Greal*, a sea serpent attacked a ship in the Menai Straits, north of Barmouth, in October 1805. Such aggressiveness is usually absent from more reliable sea monster reports. The story relates how the serpent crawled up the tiller and coiled itself around the mast. Attacked by the crew, it slithered overboard, but continued to follow the vessel for some time further. Modern monster accounts began in 1971.

Two people holidaying from Colwyn Bay were walking along the beach north of the town at Llanaber when they came across some very strange footprints, between 12 and 18 inches diameter, at the water's edge. During December 1975, the aptly named Mr Holmes from Dolgellau reportedly found prints in the sand near the Penmaenpool toll bridge. They were each larger than a dinner

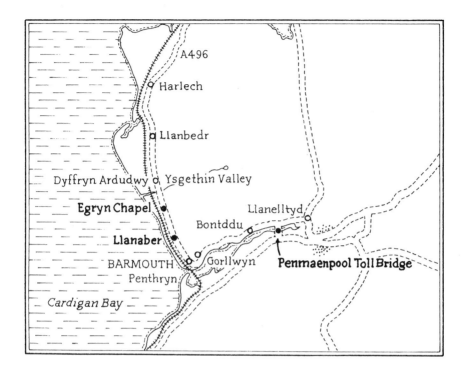

plate, and Mr Holmes had the impression they were webbed.

This was one of several incidents during that year. On 2 March six local schoolgirls had a strange experience on Barmouth beach itself. It was growing dusk when the twelve-year-olds watched a creature rise up from the beach and disappear into the sea about 200 yards away.

Julie Anderson and Carys Jones said it was about 10 feet long with a long tail and neck and had feet like huge saucers. Its skin was black but patchy-looking, and very baggy. Huge green eyes stared at them from above the waterline as it swam off. Julie Anderson's coastguard father said the girls were genuinely upset by the experience. The girls' art teacher, Colin Palmer, made a drawing based on their descriptions.

Mr Palmer was to show the drawing to the crew of a fishing boat who had been positioned off Bardsey Sound across Cardigan Bay. In calm waters the beast, or one like it, surfaced just a few yards from the boat. It repeated this manoeuvre three more times over the next hour, submerging with phenomenal speed. They

---

SEA MONSTERS WORLDWIDE

There are dozens of well-documented sightings of sea monsters. Here are a few:

* Just before the outbreak of World War II, the captain of
  British Power travelling towards Abadan in the Persian Gulf
  saw one of the creatures. The head was horse-like, perched
  on the end of a neck which was six to eight feet long.
* The west coast of Canada has provided cryptozoologists with
  many well-authenticated cases. Native Indians already had
  a tradition of monster sightings before the white man
  came. The beasts have earned the collective noun of
  'Cadborosaurus' or 'Caddy'.
* In October 1983 near Stinson Beach, north of San Francisco,
  members of a highway construction crew were the main witnesses to a beast a hundred feet long which coiled its body
  into humps.
* Chesapeake Bay cuts through the district of Columbia and
  part of Virginia. It covers an area of almost two hundred
  square miles and has produced many monster sightings over
  the years. The monster has earned the name 'Chessie'.

---

described a huge body, long neck and head, similar to the drawing.

Marjorie and Vernon Bennett were sailing their sloop a few
miles north near Harlech in the summer of that year when they
sighted something. At first they thought it was a seal playing in
two floating car tyres. As the boat drew closer they changed their
minds and speculated that it might be a huge turtle. But the nearer
they came the less sure the couple were that they could recognize
the animal.

Mrs Bennett said: 'It had a free-moving neck, fairly short, rather
like a turtle's, and an egg-shaped head about the size of a seal's. Its
back had two spines, which were sharply ridged, and it was about
8 feet across and 11 feet long, although the ripples on the water
when it dived indicated it was probably about twice that length.'

Did a sea serpent take up residence along the coast near
Barmouth in the 1970s? If so, what happened to it, and could the
beast return?

Something other than sea monsters was once seen mysteriously disappearing into Barmouth Bay. On 9 September 1922 John Morris, coxswain of the Barmouth lifeboat, and William Jones were looking out to sea when they saw what they thought was an aircraft falling very slowly into the ocean. They rushed out, expecting to find wreckage and possibly survivors, but discovered no sign of the object. No aircraft was ever reported missing.

HEAVENLY LIGHTS

Two miles north of Barmouth on the A496 is a small building known as Egryn Chapel, which played a central role during the sudden emergence of strange light phenomena at the beginning of the twentieth century. These phenomena coincided with a visit to the area of Mary Jones, who was on a Christian revivalist mission. Many people interpreted it as heavenly support for her work.

Inexplicable lights first appeared in December 1904 and continued until July 1905. They took various forms, mainly spheres and columns, and were witnessed by a large number of people, including sceptical journalists from national newspapers. One of the first incidents was an arch of light which had one foot in the sea and the other in a mountaintop about a mile inland. By January the lights were in full flood, peaking in February. It was on 11 March that the religious interpretation was reinforced.

A journalist from the *Daily Mail* had just interviewed Mary Jones at a farmhouse near Egryn and was taking a walk when he saw a ball of yellow light a few yards above the chapel roof. As he and a local man watched, it hung in the air with electric brilliance before disappearing. A few minutes later two lights appeared on either side of the chapel, about 100 feet above it. They flickered, then finally went out. Later, a yellow light appeared close by on a hillside, like 'a solid bulb of light'.

On another occasion two *Daily Mirror* staff observed lights while in Mary Jones' entourage, returning from Bontddu to Egryn.

It was close on midnight and we were nearing Barmouth, when suddenly a soft shimmering radiance flooded the road at our feet. Immediately it spread around us, and every stick and stone within twenty yards was visible. Quickly as I looked up, the light was even then fading. I seemed to see an oval mass of grey half open, disclosing within a kernel of light. As I looked it closed, and everything was once again in darkness.

There were more sightings by journalists on the road and above the chapel. On 13 March a clergyman who was hostile to Mary Jones saw an 'irregular mass of white light' heading towards Egryn Chapel. As he watched, it took the shape of a solid-looking triangle with sparkling lights in its centre. The object hovered over the roof before vanishing. A local farmer observed 'a large square of light' positioned a few feet above a mountaintop near Egryn.

Also on 13 March, Mary Jones, accompanied by a Baptist minister named H. D. Jones, were returning by car with the rest of their party from a meeting in Ty'n-y-Drain, near Llanbedr, seven miles north of Barmouth on the A496. A light 'suddenly appeared above the roadway, a few yards in front of the car, around which it played and danced'. As they reached a crossroads, the light took off towards Egryn, following the route of the party.

AN EARLIER INVASION

Although most of the sightings occurred on or from what is how the A496 near Barmouth, people reported lights from further inland too. But strange lights had invaded the area before, in the late 1820s, according to the *Mirror* of 28 August 1830. The reporter relates several experiences of local people, starting with a group approaching a ferry house at Penthryn, south of the river opposite Barmouth:

> They observed a light near a house, which they conjectured to be a bonfire, and greatly puzzled were they to discover the reason why it should have been lighted. As they came nearer, it vanished, and when they enquired at the house, they were surprised to learn that not only had the people there displayed no light, but they had not even seen one, nor could they perceive any signs of it on the sands.

On reaching Barmouth they found additional witnesses, and one of them said it was a 'death token'. Sure enough, a few nights later the ferryman drowned at the spot where the light had been seen.

The report continues with other sightings: 'The Barmouth people were struck by the appearance of a number of small lights which were seen dancing in the air. At Borthwyn [now Gorllwyn], half a mile from the town, a great number of people came out to see the lights; and after a while they all but one disappeared, and this proceeded slowly towards the water's edge, to a little bay where some boats were moored.' Some men in a sloop saw the light advancing towards them. It hovered over a boat nearby, then disappeared. According to the article, the man who owned that particular boat was also drowned a few days later. . . .

Whatever is responsible for the light phenomena – earth energies or UFOs – they seem to stop as mysteriously as they begin. This means they can start again – at any time.

ALSO NEARBY

A few miles north of Barmouth is the village of Dyffryn Ardudwy. During summer there are many organized walks from the village, one of which takes in the enchanting Ysgethin Valley which features several Neolithic burial chambers.

How to Find Barmouth

The A496 runs from Blaenau Ffestiniog down the west coast through Barmouth to Llanelltyd, just past Bontddu. Harlech Castle is a sight to behold, high above the sea, suddenly appearing out of nowhere, and nearby Shell Island is worth a visit. Why the Barmouth area should be the location for two different phenomena is intriguing, to say the least.

See map on page 199 and also consult Ordnance Survey map 124.

NEAREST MAIN TOURIST INFORMATION CENTRE
High Street, Porthmadog, Gwynedd, LL49 9LP. *Tel: 01766 512981.*

OTHER SEA MONSTERS SIGHTED OFF THE WELSH COAST

There is a dirth of recorded sea monster sightings around Wales. One good historical case comes from Llandudno on the north coast.

On Sunday 3 September 1882 a Mr F. T. Mott in the company of Mr W. Barfoot, a JP, and solicitor Mr F. J. Marlow, were standing on the pier passing the time of day. Suddenly they saw a black snake-like creature swimming across the mouth of the bay towards the Great Orme.

The observation lasted about two minutes and during that time they estimated the creature's length as around two hundred foot. An account was published in the prestigious journal *Nature*. Mr Barfoot answered criticisms by stating his wide experience of the sea, and conjecturing that the phenomenon the three men had observed could not be accounted for by known species of sea life.

THE BROAD HAVEN INVASION

HYSTERIA OR PHENOMENA?

*A*CCORDING TO DOZENS of reliable eye-witness reports, around 1977 the area in and about Broad Haven in West Wales was visited by UFOs and strange beings. The incidents were written up in three books: *The Dyfed Enigma* by Randall Jones Pugh and F. W. Holiday, *The Welsh Triangle* by Peter Paget and *The Uninvited* by Clive Harold. Did a wave of hysteria wash over the community, or was Broad Haven the focus for phenomena from elsewhere?

The hills around the village slope towards a wide, sandy beach. Folded cliffs rise to either side commanding a view over St Bride's Bay, the location for spectacular summer sunsets and other, less natural, phenomena. This unspoilt beauty is protected by the Pembrokeshire Coast National Park. Although new property has been added in recent years, the original Victorian atmosphere survives in places like Webbs Hill and Trafalgar Terrace. The National Park Information Centre stands on a large car park set back from the beach.

There had already been a number of strange incidents when, on 4 February 1977, the children of Broad Haven County Primary School became embroiled. The school lies at the southern end of the village, at the bottom of Marine Road.

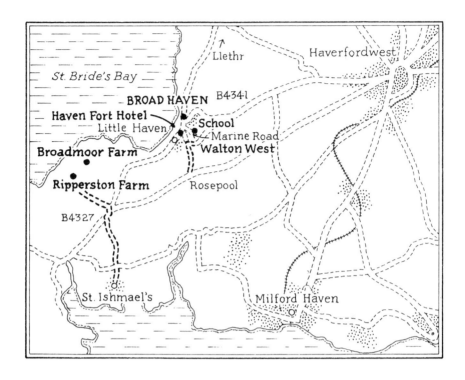

MR SPOCK AT BROAD HAVEN

Fourteen children, aged between nine and eleven, were in the playground after lunch when one of them spotted a strange-looking object in a field behind the school. It was a silvery yellow colour, cigar-shaped, with a dome on top, and moving slowly about. A few thought they saw a figure nearby. Eleven-year-old Michael Webb, the son of an RAF Squadron Leader, offered this description: 'When I first looked at it, it looked like two ordinary saucers put one against each other, to make a sort of dome. Then you've got a small ashtray, put on top, and that makes another sort of dome on top. And I thought I saw windows – about three or four round the edge on top of the dome. And a light flashing on top.'

David George, aged nine, was one child who thought he saw a figure. He described the humanoid as 'a silver man with spiked ears' – sounding like Mr Spock from *Star Trek!* Several of the children said the object shimmered at one point, and seemed to be having difficulty lifting off from the ground.

When some of the boys went to see the headmaster, Ralph Llewellyn, and told him what they had seen, he declined to go and look, thinking perhaps it was a prank. That afternoon after school one of the witnesses, a boy named David Davies, told his mother about the object. She was so convinced by the account that she telephoned local UFO investigator Randall Jones Pugh.

The following day Pugh and a local journalist went to the 'landing' site but found nothing unusual. By Monday the headmaster realized that something strange really had happened. He separated the children who had seen the object from the other pupils, and asked them to draw the UFO and describe what they had seen. After the story appeared in the newspapers, the children were interviewed extensively. The interviewers came away convinced the sighting was not a hoax, but wondered if there could be a normal explanation. Thirteen days from the first sighting, the UFO returned – and this time the witnesses were not children.

ADULT WITNESSES

A teacher leaving the school by a side entrance at 10.30 a.m. saw in the field 'a large object, oval-shaped, with a slight dome'. It made a humming noise and glided behind some trees.

Later that same day two women who worked in the school kitchen saw an object on the ground. As they watched, a figure climbed into the machine and it moved up a slope out of sight. As it was raining, and difficult to see clearly, they decided it must have been a council truck moving sewage.

They reported it to Mr Llewellyn, but he thought it was an unlikely explanation. The ground was too boggy where the women had observed the object, but they still thought this was what they had seen. The following day the women went with their husbands to the location. The group found themselves floundering in a foot-deep bog, and Randall Jones Pugh was subsequently informed by the council that no lorry had been near the field.

UNUSUAL VISITORS AT THE HAVEN FORT HOTEL

The Haven Fort Hotel lies just outside Broad Haven along the coastal road which leads to nearby Little Haven. The hotel is a converted seventeenth-century fortification, built on the site of an even older habitation. In 1970 the Granville family took over the business, along with its resident ghostly 'white lady'. But what Mrs Rose Granville experienced during the early hours of 19 April 1977 had nothing to do with the resident apparition.

She went to bed at about 2 a.m. and became aware of a humming noise. Thinking she had left the central heating system on, Rose went to investigate. The heating was off. Could it be a ship in the bay, was her next thought. She opened the curtains, and was surprised to see a blue light in the field next to the hotel.

Rose wondered if someone was trying to break into a cottage she owned nearby, and picked up her binoculars for a better look. The light came from an oval object resting on the ground. There were two figures standing nearby with pointed heads. They were between six and a half and seven feet tall, and clothed in whitish 'boiler suits'. Their arms and legs were very long, similar to a gibbon's. As far as she could tell in the blue light, their faces were featureless.

Mrs Granville tried to call out to her husband, but found she was speechless. In panic she ran round the hotel, switching all the lights on. When she looked again, the object and the humanoids had gone. The following day she found an oval impression on the ground, but a later inspection by Pugh and his colleague F. W. Holiday revealed nothing. However, radiation readings taken at the site a year later by my colleague Dr Harry Hudson showed higher than normal levels. Ironically, the site was 120 yards from the hotel and near to an atomic bomb shelter belonging to the Ministry of Defence, which Pugh and Holiday speculated the beings might have been interested in inspecting.

Rose Granville told me: 'The sightings were a complete mystery to us, and to this day we are unsure of their origin. Some people have suggested they were extraterrestrial beings, while others say it could have been connected with the military. Whatever, it was a very strange experience!'

UFO CATTLE RUSTLERS AT RIPPERSTON FARM

About three miles south of Broad Haven lies Ripperston Farm. This was the focus for a concentration of UFO and humanoid sightings, including the bizarre teleportation of livestock. It centred around the Coombes family. Billie Coombes, head dairyman, lived at the farm with his wife Pauline and their five children.

Pauline was driving back to Ripperston from St Ishmaels after taking home a boy who had visited the farm. She had three of the children with her. As they reached the B4327 her son pointed out an object in the sky which was approaching the car. It shone yellow and was about the shape of a rugby ball. As they went on to the minor road which led to the farm they could see that the object was pacing the car at the side of them. When the vehicle reached the house the lights dimmed and the engine cut out. Billie Coombes came out in time to observe the object heading seawards.

TELEPORTATION

Teleportation was a term invented by Charles Fort to describe the movement of people or objects over distances without physical aid.

- In 1593 a Spanish soldier stationed in the Philippines suddenly appeared in Mexico City, 9,000 miles away.
- Between the years of 1620–1631 the Venerable Mary of Jesus teleported over 500 times from her Spanish convent to New Mexico, where she converted the Jumano Indians. This was confirmed in writing by missionaries who wrote to the Pope and Philip IV.
- Most alleged cases of teleportation occur spontaneously. In May 1968, Dr Gerald Vidal and his wife were teleported in their car from Agentina to Mexico, thousands of miles away.

The Coombes then began having trouble with their cattle, which were kept locked up at night behind a gate reinforced with twine to stop the bolt accidentally moving. On several occasions a herd of a hundred cattle got out of the yard and was found at Lower Broadmoor Farm about half a mile away. They did this without being seen or heard – even by the farm dog. Further, the gate was still locked exactly as Billie had left it. Over this period the animals seemed very restless and gave a poor milk yield.

On 15 April the phenomenon even occurred in daylight. Sixteen heifers disappeared from their secured pen in the space of four minutes. Impossible though it seems, they too were found at Broadmoor Farm.

Things came to a head on the evening of 22 April. Earlier in the evening there had been a lot of television interference and a power cut. The television set was positioned under a window where the curtains were not drawn. At 11.30 p.m. Pauline noticed a silvery glow outside, but ignored it and continued to watch the pro-gramme. At 1.50 a.m. Billie suddenly leaped up, exclaiming; 'What the hell's that?' They saw a 'man' pressed up against the glass, wearing a silver suit, almost seven feet tall. Although he had a face, it lacked any features. Even while Pauline was phoning for the police, the bizarre figure was still standing there. It disappeared shortly before officers arrived.

There were more sightings of the strange figure, and other odd things happened around the farm and Broad Haven in the months to come. The phenomenon widened its interests to include the vil-lages around Milford Haven and Haverfordwest, then seemed to stop as suddenly as it started. What was the explanation? 'Rational' theories did not seem to fit most of the cases. Pugh and Holiday noted that a number of leys cut through many of the loca-tions where things had happened. Was there a disruption in these energy lines that allowed things from a parallel reality to enter ours temporarily? If so, could it happen again?

OTHER INCIDENTS NEAR BROAD HAVEN

9 December 1976: Ethel Cale, Nicholas Cale, Mrs Yvonne Andrews and Mrs Anne Berry were travelling from Broad Haven to Milford Haven. On the road between Walton West and Rosepool they saw a dome-shaped, bright flashing light above the hedge on the left-hand side of the road.

13 March 1977: Seventeen-year-old Stephen Taylor was walking home to Llethr, eight miles north of Broad Haven, from his girlfriend's house at 9 p.m. when he noticed a glowing oval object over Hendre Bridge. Later, he saw a black dog racing away from the scene. At 9.30 p.m. he had reached the perimeter fence to Brawdy NATO airbase. There he saw a dome-shaped vehicle just over a fence. As he went to look he was startled by the arrival of a tall 'man'. The humanoid wore a one-piece suit and had a tube going into his mouth. He had a large black eyes, like those of a fish, and high cheekbones. Stephen was so afraid that he lashed out at the figure, but felt nothing. The teenager turned and ran.

26 March 1977: Josephine Hewison, manager of Lower Broadmoor Farm, glanced out of her bedroom window at about 7.50 a.m. She wondered why she could not see the large greenhouse about 100 yards away. Then she realized there was something parked in front of it. The aluminium-coloured object was dome-shaped and in three tiers, 35–40 feet wide. She went and awoke her three sons, but when she returned with them to the window the object had gone.

27 April 1977: Broad Haven garage proprieter John Davies and his wife observed a light from the beach. It moved about the moonlit sky in short bursts before disappearing.

6 May 1977: Ms E. Griffiths, who lived at Holme Dean, Walton West, just half a mile from Broad Haven Primary School, was surprised to see from her kitchen window a bright silver 'car' in the middle of a cornfield. It suddenly vanished, to reappear in another part of the field. The object did this several times. Investigators found damage in the field, but it was not possible to say what had caused it.

25 June 1977: In the early hours Ministry of Defence electrician Stephen Bamford and a group of other observers, which included local authority technician Robert Best, saw a strange phenomenon from the sea front. It was an orange 'oscillating' object which emerged from Stack Rock, half a mile away, then seemed to shrink into nothing.

How to Find Broad Haven

From Carmarthen take the A40 to Haverfordwest and then join the B4341 which leads into the village. The Haven Fort Hotel at Little Haven offers bed and breakfast accommodation. *Tel: 0437 781401.*
Consult Ordnance Survey map 157.

NEAREST MAIN TOURIST INFORMATION CENTRE
Old Bridge, Haverfordwest, Pembrokeshire, Dyfed, SA61 2EZ. *Tel: 01437 763110.*

OTHER UFO CLOSE ENCOUNTER CASES IN WALES

On the evening of 1 September 1978, the village of Llaner-chymedd was thrown into uproar. Llanerchymedd is on the island of Anglesey in Gwynedd where the B5112 and the B5111 meet. Some boys were playing football on the edge of the village at dusk when they noticed a 'helicopter' landing in a nearby field. When they went to look they found a white bullet-shaped object resting vertically on the ground surrounded by a reddish glow.

People in nearby houses also saw the landing. The boys went and fetched two women before returning to the field. In the fading light they saw two six-foot figures in hooded one-piece suits. Many witnesses later came forward to confirm that they too had seen the object. In the panic no one observed it leave.

The police were called and it was speculated that the incident had something to do with nearby RAF Valley, but they denied all knowledge. Investigators discovered that barley had been flattened into a circle where the 'object' had landed.

A year earlier on 14 December Carl Hollins, a light aircraft pilot, took off from Liverpool Airport for Llandwrog. While flying over Mount Snowdon, Hollins claims to have encountered a multi-faceted black object that seemed to play cat and mouse with him before disappearing in cloud. Hollins told me he landed at RAF Valley to report the incident, but I could obtain no proof of this from the MoD seven years later.

Resources

ORGANISATIONS AND JOURNALS

Always send a stamped addressed envelope when making enquiries of any of the following.

Association for the Scientific Study of Anomalous Phenomena: Hugh Pincott, ASSAP Secretary, 20 Paul Street, Frome, Somerset, BA11 1DX.

Northern Anomalies Research Association: Margaret Holt, NARO Secretary, 2 Grosvenor Road, Congleton, Cheshire, CW12 4PG. Please note that NARO only recruits members able to attend regular meetings in Manchester.

Strange Phenomena Investigations: Malcolm Robinson, 41 The Braes, Tullibody, Clackmannanshire, Scotland, FK10 2TT. The paranormal journal *Enigmas* is published by SPI and well worth subscribing to.

Northern UFO News, Jenny Randles, Editor, 37 Heathbank Road, Cheadle Heath, Stockport, Cheshire, SK3 OUP.

BOOKS AND PARTWORKS

AA Book of British Villages (Drive Publications Ltd 1980)
Ashe, Geoffrey, *Mythology of the British Isles* (Methuen 1990)
Baldwin, Gay, *More Ghosts of the Isle of Wight* (available from the author; telephone 0983 294651)
Baldwin, Gay, *Ghosts of the Isle of Wight III* (Ensign 1994)
Bord, Janet and Colin, *Alien Animals* (Granada 1980)
Bord, Janet and Colin *Atlas of Magical Britain* (Sidgwick & Jackson 1990)
Bord, Janet and Colin, *Sacred Waters* (Paladin 1986)
Brooks, J.A., *Ghosts and Witches of the Cotswolds* (Jarrold 1986)
Brooksmith, Peter (ed.), *The Unexplained* (Orbis partwork 1980–3)
Castleden, Rodney, *The Wilmington Giant: The Quest for a Lost Myth* (Turnstone Press 1984)
Cavendish, Richard (ed.), *Man, Myth and Magic* (Purnell partwork 1970)
Clarke, David, *Strange South Yorkshire* (Sigma Press 1994)
Copper, Basil, *The Vampire in Legend, Fact and Fiction* (Hale 1990)
Devereux, Paul, *Earth Lights Revelation* (Blandford 1990)
Dinsdale, Tim, *The Story of the Loch Ness Monster* (Target 1974)
Fort, Charles, *The Complete Books* (Dover Publications 1974)
Goss, Michael, *The Evidence for Phantom Hitch-Hikers* (Aquarian 1984)
Harold, Clive, *The Uninvited* (Nelson 1981, now out of print)
Hough, Peter, *Witchcraft: A Strange Conflict* (Lutterworth 1991)

Hough, Peter and Randles, Jenny, *Mysteries of the Mersey Valley* (Sigma 1993)

Hough, Peter and Randles, Jenny, *The Complete Book of UFOs* (Piatkus 1994)

Johnson, Frank, *The Janos People* (Spearman 1980)

Paget, Peter, *The Welsh Triangle* (Panther 1979, now out of print)

Palmer, Geoffrey and Lloyd, Noel, *A Year of Festivals* (Warne 1972)

Pugh, Randall Jones and Holiday, F. W. *The Dyfed Enigma* (Faber & Faber 1979)

Randles, Jenny, *Pennine UFO Mystery* (Granada 1983)

Randles, Jenny, *UFO Study* (Hale 1981)

Randles, Jenny and Fuller, Paul, *Crop Circles: A Mystery Solved* (Hale 1990)

Randles, Jenny, *From Out of the Blue* (Global Communications 1991)

Randles, Jenny and Hough, Peter, *Death by Supernatural Causes* (Grafton 1988)

Randles, Jenny and Hough, Peter, *The Afterlife* (Piatkus 1993)

Randles, Jenny and Hough, Peter, *The Encyclopedia of the Unexplained* (Michael O'Mara Ltd 1994)

Shuttleworth, Arthur, *The Warminster Mystery* (Tandem 1976)

Stoker, Bram, *Dracula* (Foulsham 1986)

Wilson, Colin, *Poltergeist!* (NEL 1981)

BOOKLETS, JOURNALS, ARTICLES, LEAFLETS ETC

AA Big Road Atlas of Britain (Automobile Association 1992)

Alderley Edge Official Guide (published by Alderley Edge Parish Council, available through local Tourist Information Centres)

Borley Parish Church (booklet published by the church and compiled by several writers)

Carlyon, Kevin, 'Results of Wilmington Telepathy Tests,' *Exploring the Supernatural*, January 1987

Edwards, W. Le Cato, *Epworth: The Home of the Wesleys* (published by author)

Enigmas, journal of Strange Phenomena Investigations (SPI), edited by Malcolm Robinson. Issues 31, 32, 33 and 35 contain articles on Bonnybridge UFO encounters

Farrant, David, 'The Hooded Spectre of Netley Abbey', *The Unknown*, June 1987

Halliday, Ron, 'Dowsing at Loch Morar', *Enigmas*, No. 25 August/September 1991

Leslie, Desmond, 'The Coniston Saucer', *The Outspan*, 25 June 1954

Lewis, Michael, 'Ghostly Alarm at the Inn', *ASSAP News*, No. 46, February 1993

Lewis, Michael, 'Ram Inn UpDate', *ASSAP News*, No. 48, August 1993

Llafar Gwlad 'Bala Lake Monster' (Welsh journal published in April 1991)

London A – Z (Geographers' A – Z Map Co. Ltd)

McDermott, Paul, *The Whitby Ghost Book* (Anderson Publications 1990)

Paths Around Pendle (contains a map with tourist and historical information published by Duncan Armstrong & Associates of Padiham)

Russell, Barbara, 'Report of an All Night Vigil at an Inn', *Anomaly*, Issue 7, 1990.

Waters, Colin, *Whitby and the Dracula Connection* (Whitby Press)

Waters, Colin, *Bygone Whitby* (Anderson Publications 1988)

Yuille, Judith, *The Landscape of Highgate Cemetery* (leaflet published by the friends of Highgate Cemetery)

Index of Place Names